THE UNICORN FALLACY

THE
UNICORN
FALLACY

DITCH THE GROWTH-OR-DIE HERD
AND BUILD A COMPANY THAT LASTS

CHRIS CABRERA

LIONCREST
PUBLISHING

THE UNICORN FALLACY
Ditch the Growth-or-Die Herd and Build a Company That Lasts

FIRST EDITION

ISBN   978-1-5445-4497-7   *Hardcover*
       978-1-5445-4496-0   *Paperback*
       978-1-5445-4495-3   *Ebook*

I would like to dedicate this book to my wife and love of my life, Marla. For thirty-three years Marla has been by my side, through great times and also through challenging times. She has helped guide me through every major decision and has always encouraged me. She lifts me when I have been down and has kept me centered amidst it all—meaning she can slap me into line and will not tolerate anything but my best. I am eternally grateful not only to have her as my wife, but as my truest and best friend.

CONTENTS

INTRODUCTION

WE'RE ALL IN THE SAME STORM

"THINGS ARE GOING GREAT. WE'RE ABSOLUTELY CRUSHING it right now."

I wasn't expecting my friend to answer my question so enthusiastically—especially since Xactly, the company I ran, was decidedly *not* crushing it.

I couldn't square the difference. On the face of things, our companies were very similar. We were both in the software-as-a-service (SaaS) business, we both catered to a similar clientele, and we both managed similarly sized workforces.

And yet, despite all these similarities, our experiences in the market couldn't have been more different.

While he was killing it, we were in the middle of a nasty storm. None of our buyers wanted to make any decisions. They all kept pushing out. We couldn't get them over the finish line. As a result, we'd just come out of our second rough quarter in a row—with no end in sight.

I ended the call and sat staring at the wall. What was going on here? How could we be struggling while his company seemed to be thriving? Were we doing something wrong? Was there some weird quirk in the market? Were we not as strong of a company as I thought we were?

Perhaps not.

A few months later, I got a call from that same CEO friend. This time, when I asked him how things were going, he was singing a much different tune. "Terrible," he said. "Everything you told me about your last quarter is happening to us this quarter!"

They weren't hitting their numbers. Their sales reps weren't happy. They were having a tough time paying their bills. Prices were going up. And to top it all off, their best people were *quitting*.

"It's a nightmare!" my friend exclaimed.

My friend wasn't the only business leader to describe a sudden change in fortunes. After all, we're living in especially volatile times. In just the few years leading up to the publication of this book, this business world has been rocked by storm after storm. First, there was the COVID-19 pandemic, then there was the Great Resignation, then there was the massive spike in inflation, and so on.

Each storm brought new challenges—challenges that I naively assumed everyone was experiencing in the same way. Same storm, same problems, right?

But after speaking with my friend—and many other business leaders like him—I realized I was wrong. Yes, we all navigated the same storms, but we were in different boats.

We each experience every new storm in a different way. If you're a small business, even a small storm could seem catastrophic when compared to the experience of a larger business. Sometimes, a large storm could devastate a larger business but leave their smaller counterparts unscathed.

That's why I love asking business leaders how things are going in their company. Not to compare our own relative success to theirs, but to see how they're weathering the current storm—and to see whether they're prepared for the next one.

Unfortunately, I've discovered that very few are.

RUDDERLESS AND ADRIFT

If you're reading this book, it's because, quite frankly, you're rudderless in the storm.

Maybe you're lost at sea in a market that rapidly expanded and then contracted around your business.

Maybe you went all in on growth and are now faced with an economy that no longer supports such a gung-ho approach.

Maybe you've played it safe and focused on building a quality business but have recently begun to suspect that the traditional ways of doing so are starting to feel outdated.

Whatever the case, you aren't sure how to weather the storm currently facing your business. You haven't failed, but you're not doing as well as you'd like either. Something has to change.

Here's the good news. Yes, each storm may be different. Yes, each storm may bring unique challenges. But the best way to navigate your company out of any storm is almost always the same: focus on building a quality, sustainable business.

I know what you're thinking: *No shit, Chris. We're all trying to do that.*

Fair point.

We're all trying to build great businesses. In all my years interacting with other business leaders, I've yet to meet someone who didn't genuinely want to build a quality business.

But I've met far fewer who actually believe they're doing it. Most likely, you're one of them.

Don't believe me? Here, I'll prove it.

Look at the current state of your revenue operation. Do you trust your numbers? Do you trust your product? Do you trust your market? When you look at your sales engine, do you see a well-oiled machine, or do you see a thousand unknown, undefined problems that could capsize your whole operation?

If you answered yes to any of those questions, then there's your problem: you don't have a quality revenue operation. To create a quality business, focus on quality revenue.

Yes, there's more to building a quality business than just revenue alone. You also need to deliver a quality product, support your organization with the right systems and structure, and grow a winning organizational culture. Those are all important things—and I certainly encourage you not to ignore them. However, without revenue, any other initiative you might be considering is dead in the water.

A quality revenue operation is the engine that drives the rest of your business. However, most organizations don't give their revenue operation the attention it deserves.

That's too bad.

First, building a quality revenue engine—just like building a quality organization—is an evergreen move that makes sense in any economic climate for any company. In a bullish, investor-friendly climate, a quality revenue operation will only improve your valuation. In a bearish climate, it will help you demonstrate that you are both stable and profitable.

Second, a lot has changed in the world of revenue—both in terms of how leaders think about it and the tools they use to drive it. It's no longer enough to chase the most revenue, to grow at all costs even if you aren't profitable. It's no longer enough to manage complex (and costly) revenue calculations on clumsy, error-prone spreadsheets. It's no longer enough to blindly call the ball on your forecasts and white-knuckle it through the year to see if you were right. Those approaches might have worked for your predecessors, but today, we have the technology and tactics to push well beyond that.

How do I know? Because at Xactly, the company I founded with Satish K. Palvai in 2005, we're leading the charge. A better way is possible, and we've made it our mission to revolutionize the way businesses manage the revenue arm of their business through an approach we call *Intelligent Revenue.*

At its core, Intelligent Revenue comes down to three things: tech, tactics, and alignment. With robust data and machine learning tools, today's organizations can generate unprecedented insights into how they're generating revenue. Then, with the right tactics, these organizations can work to maximize value at every step. Of course, all the tech and tactics in the world won't amount to much if your people aren't on board with the plan—which is why alignment is crucial to any effective revenue operation.

This is the rudder you're looking for to stabilize your ship. Sure, every organization is different and has different needs. However, the fundamentals of a healthy revenue operation are largely the same for any company. Master those fundamentals, and you will position your business to weather any storm.

That doesn't mean giving up on your dream business, but shifting to a concept that's more stable. Such a shift can be difficult to wrap your head around. I would know. For a long time, I was in the exact same boat.

DON'T LET THE GAME PLAY YOU

At this point, some of you reading this may be feeling a bit blindsided. Most likely, you've been playing the game you thought you were supposed to play, racing after that billion-dollar valuation with a growth-at-all-costs strategy so you could attract as many investors as possible and achieve *unicorn* status in the business world.

If you're one of those readers, I get it. There's an aspiring unicorn in all of us, even if, as we'll discuss in Chapter 1, being a unicorn isn't all it's cracked up to be.

The truth is, I used to chase the unicorn dream too—in fact, I was *encouraged* to. I was the CEO of Xactly for fifteen years before anyone asked me about our company's EBITDA (earnings before interest, taxes, depreciation, and amortization). All our investors wanted us to do was grow, grow, grow—so that's precisely what we did.

If I'm being honest, this growth-at-all-costs approach never sat well with me. In fact, in many ways, it went directly against what I had come to know and value.

My father was an entrepreneur who immigrated from Colombia and had a thick accent. Some people had trouble understanding him at times, but he cared about the people he employed and worked tirelessly to show it. I still remember riding along with him every year on the day before Thanksgiving as he delivered turkeys to all of his employees.

Through my father, I learned the importance of putting people first. He was a master at this, even if he wasn't quite as shrewd when it came to growing his business, where he took a far more conservative approach. Rather than seek financing to grow his operation, he bootstrapped everything. This led to a feast-or-famine childhood for me and prevented him from taking his business to the next level.

My father may have thought financing was a four-letter word, but business school taught me differently. Perhaps more importantly, though, it taught me that my father wasn't entirely wrong.

There is a right way and a wrong way to pursue financing—and a growth-at-all-costs strategy was firmly in the "wrong" camp. While that aggressive approach worked for some, it was disastrous to most.

If only I had listened.

When I first founded Xactly in 2005, and for several years afterward, we aggressively pursued a growth-or-die strategy in order to attract investors and raise capital. In some ways, we had little choice. Especially at the time, all our investors wanted to talk about was growth. Growth got them larger valuations, which in turn put them in a position to turn a profit on their investment more quickly.

And so, best practices be damned, Xactly played the game and gave our investors the growth they desired. But I also never gave up on what I knew was right. I didn't just want a business that grew. I wanted a business that was *profitable*. So, outside of a few growth-intensive years, we worked to build a business that would last.

Then the market shifted, and the game changed.

Overnight, all those would-be unicorn companies—dozens of them—that had received billion-dollar valuations were struggling. They couldn't earn a profit, and they couldn't deliver what they promised. As a result, they couldn't attract new investors. Because they had raised money on outsized valuations, raising additional money would result in a massive down round.

Even Xactly—which *was* a profitable company—felt this shift. In 2021, we reported 86 percent growth at our company. Just a few years prior, that number would have investors salivating. Instead, they all came back to us with the same concern: Where was the profit to match?

Since founding Xactly, that was the first time I'd ever heard an investor ask that question. Finally, after all these years, investors were speaking my language.

Sure, it meant that we had a ways to go to convince these investors that we were, in fact, a profitable company. However, because we had always been at least somewhat focused on building a quality company with a sustainable, Intelligent Revenue operation, we were far better positioned to weather the storm than many competing organizations.

For many of those organizations, the early years of the 2020s have been a humbling experience, to say the least. As a friend to many of their leaders, it was painful to watch. For years, these companies had been cruising in the unicorn fast lane, chasing higher and higher valuations to secure an ever-growing share of venture capital (VC) money. And then, all momentum came screeching to a halt. With no more investors, these CEOs all became obsessed with the same thing: retaining capital.

All they needed now was a plan.

REINVENT YOURSELF

The Intelligent Revenue framework outlined in this book is designed to help any organization build a predictable, stable, and sustainable revenue engine. This is not a strategy for doubling down on a growth-at-all-costs strategy, although many of the practices outlined in this book will absolutely help you grow your business.

But if growth is all you're after, then I'm sorry to say this, but you've fallen for the *Unicorn Fallacy*—and eventually, you're going to wind up extinct.

There's a reason why only about 25 percent of founders are still the CEOs of their companies by the time they go public: they fail to transition from startup mode and focus on long-term success.[1] Growth is an important strategy when you're trying to get your first five clients. If you'd like to stick around for a while, though, eventually you'll have to turn your attention to building a great business.

If you're already focused on building a quality business, then two things. First, hallelujah, you're ahead of the curve! Second, don't let up on the gas. Here is your chance to get your revenue engine running at peak potential.

To help you get the most out of this book, I've divided it into two parts.

- **Part 1: The Case for Intelligent Revenue.** Here, we begin by diving deeper into the Unicorn Fallacy and why the go-for-growth mindset is so destructive for business leaders. Then we'll introduce the concept of Intelligent Revenue, discussing how technology, tactics, and alignment work in synergy to bolster a thriving revenue engine.
- **Part 2: Optimizing for Growth and Sustainability.** Here's where the rubber hits the road. In Part 2, we'll walk you through specific, actionable principles for you to apply an Intelligent Revenue model to the different levers of your revenue operation.

As you move through these chapters, one last note on how to get the most value out of this book: Intelligent Revenue isn't about using new tools to do what you've always done. Just because something worked for you in the past doesn't mean it will work in the future. In fact, it likely won't.

This is a book for building the revenue engine of the future,

---

1   Noam Wasserman, "The Founder's Dilemma," *Harvard Business Review*, February 2008, https://hbr.org/2008/02/the-founders-dilemma.

not for paving the cow paths. That engine will depend on new tools, new tactics, and, most importantly, a willingness to abandon the growth-at-all-costs mindset and reinvent yourself.

If you're ready to ditch the herd and try something new, let's get started.

INTELLIGENT REVENUE TUNE-UP

In addition to providing you with helpful frameworks, practices, and examples in every chapter, I've also included a series of questions at the end of each chapter. Use these questions to tune up your Intelligent Revenue efforts and get clarity on what areas of your business are in need of direct action.

→   How are things going with your business, really?

→   How confident are you that your ship is capable of weathering the next storm?

→   Do you have systems in place to measure not only the quantity of your revenue but also the quality?

PART I

THE CASE FOR INTELLIGENT REVENUE

CHAPTER 1

THE UNICORN FALLACY

I REMEMBER WHEN UNICORNS WERE RARE.

I remember when companies were supposed to be profitable.

I remember when what you sold mattered just as much as how much of it you sold.

So, what happened?

It all started when venture capitalist Aileen Lee coined the term "unicorn startup" in 2013, a term she used to describe companies like Facebook and Google, who underwent explosive growth in a short amount of time and saw their valuations shoot past $1 billion.[2] While Lee referred to this exclusive group as a "club," she may as well have called them a herd—because suddenly every company and their mother set their sights on becoming the next unicorn so they could join the in crowd.

Over the next decade, the number of unicorns exploded from

---

2   Aileen Lee, "Welcome to the Unicorn Club: Learning from Billion-Dollar Startups," Tech Crunch, November 13, 2013, https://techcrunch.com/2013/11/02/welcome-to-the-unicorn-club/.

thirty-nine in 2013 to nearly nine hundred (and counting!) in 2022, with a combined valuation of $3.5 trillion. Unicorns have become so prevalent, in fact, that according to HubSpot, they even have their own hierarchy now; *decacorns* describe companies valued at over $10 billion, while *hectacorns* describe companies valued at over $100 billion.[3]

For most of the twenty-first century, the business world has promoted the unicorn as the ultimate ideal that all companies should aspire to. Whether it was in their best interests or not, countless business leaders heeded this call.

But was this wise? Is unicorn status truly the pinnacle of achievement, or is it a dangerous myth that harms more businesses than it helps?

In my experience, it's the latter. Detonating the unicorn myth is the most efficient way to illustrate the dangers of a growth-at-all-costs approach while also outlining why it's better (and more sustainable) to focus on building a quality business instead.

BEING A UNICORN ISN'T ALL IT'S CRACKED UP TO BE

Have you ever thought about why businesses with high valuations are called unicorns?

In some ways, it's strange. First off, unicorns aren't real. Sure, there was the "Siberian unicorn," *Elasmotherium sibiricum*, which roamed Eastern Europe near modern-day Kazakhstan, but it had more in common with a rhinoceros than with its traditional depiction in pop culture.[4] The elegant, horse-like

---

3   HubSpot, "The Comprehensive Unicorn Startup List for 2022," accessed September 8, 2023, https://www.hubspot.com/startups/unicorn-startups.

4   National Geographic Kids, "Ancient 'Unicorns' May Have Roamed Earth with Humans!," accessed April 25, 2023, https://www.natgeokids.com/uk/discover/animals/prehistoric-animals/siberian-unicorn-fossil-discovery-humans/.

creature that now dominates our collective consciousness only exists in fiction.

Here's where you start to see the appeal of the unicorn to modern-day businesses. In almost any version of the unicorn myth, unicorns and their horns are depicted as a symbol of strength and vitality. The Greek historian Ctesias claimed that unicorn horns had restorative powers. According to *Britannica*, "Those who drank from its horn were thought to be protected from stomach trouble, epilepsy, and poison."[5] Not only was it strong, but it was elusive—so elusive, in fact, that only the "purest" in society could capture it. In another Greek writing, the *Physiologus*, it was said that a unicorn could only be caught "if a virgin maiden was placed before it."[6]

All in all, the mythological unicorn is quite an impressive animal—strong, independent, pure, and even possessing healing properties. It's also incredibly rare; in the business world, the term *unicorn* was originally coined to describe how difficult it was to attain a billion-dollar valuation. Whether in business or in fiction, few were considered privileged enough to actually encounter a real-life unicorn.

When you put it that way, what business wouldn't enthusiastically pursue unicorn status? Every leader I know wants to be associated with strength and independence. As for the unicorn's rarity? Well, we all like to feel as if we're part of some exclusive club, right?

Unfortunately, this desire to be in rarefied company—to be among the few elite businesses to achieve that fabled billion-

---

5 *Encyclopaedia Britannica Online*, s.v. "unicorn," last modified August 29, 2023, https://www.britannica.com/topic/unicorn.

6 *Encyclopaedia Britannica Online*, s.v. "unicorn."

dollar valuation—became all that mattered, and business leaders began to obsess about attaining unicorn status.

There's one major problem with this approach: it's a short leap from *rare* to *extinct*. Especially in modern stories like *The Last Unicorn*, extinction is a prominent theme in unicorn mythology. Doesn't that sound familiar? Where unicorns once roamed in great numbers, they began to be hunted once humans became aware of their magical properties. As majestic as they were, they couldn't protect themselves from being killed off because they lacked adequate defenses.

Even with the explosion of unicorn companies in the 2010s and early 2020s, attaining unicorn status is still incredibly rare. As of 2022, only 0.00006 percent of all companies actually attain unicorn status.[7] But as we all know, getting there is only half the battle—and it often comes at tremendous cost. Startups like Airbnb and Uber each took on over a billion dollars in debt just to attain unicorn status.[8] For far too many startups, then, landing that big valuation means taking on tremendous financial risk, all while leaving yourself relatively unprotected in the process. It's no wonder, then, that 99.9 percent of aspiring unicorns fail to generate a meaningful (10X) return for their venture capital investors.[9]

That didn't stop them from trying anyway—and from ignoring the extinction-level reckoning to come. In the years immediately following COVID-19's peak in 2021, these ill-prepared companies fell prey to rapidly changing market

7   Sakshi Bharari, "How Does a Startup Become a Unicorn?," Business Outreach, March 25, 2023, https://www.businessoutreach.in/how-does-a-startup-become-an-unicorn/.

8   Embroker Team, "106 Must-Know Startup Statistics for 2023," Embroker, August 17, 2023, https://www.embroker.com/blog/startup-statistics/.

9   Patrick Ward, "Is It True That 90% of Startups Fail?" NanoGlobals, June 29, 2021, https://nanoglobals.com/startup-failure-rate-myths-origin/.

conditions. Unicorns still exist today, but they're no longer seen as the proud, majestic pinnacle of business they once were. These days, they're just seen as one-trick ponies on the brink of extinction.

All these one-trick ponies know how to do is sell on quantity, go all out for the big, splashy deals without considering which approaches are actually best for their company. They're proud of their unicorn-in-waiting status, despite the fact this entire strategy is named after an animal that failed to adapt to changing conditions and ultimately went *extinct*.

This mindset filters directly into the sales arm of a company, where reps who are early in their careers and eager to make a splash put all their energy into landing those home-run deals—which is fine. You need some of that in every company.

But swinging for the fences is a high-risk pursuit. If it works out, you're a hero. But if it doesn't, then eventually, at the end of the quarter, many of these sales reps—and by extension, the companies they represent—find themselves holding the bag. The sales didn't close, and they're left with nothing.

These companies fell prey to the Unicorn Fallacy. But when you pursue an unbalanced business strategy for too long, eventually you have to pay the piper.

Risk is necessary, but balance is important. It's okay to chase home runs, but you'd better scatter some singles and doubles in there too. There must be something stable to fall back on. Otherwise, like the unicorn, you'll find yourself on the verge of extinction.

This is exactly what began to happen in 2020, when, due in part to the onset of the COVID-19 pandemic and in part to other market forces already underway, the economy changed. With recession fears rampant and inflation at a forty-year high, suddenly, Xactly and many other companies caught up in the unicorn game began to realize just how much risk they were exposing themselves to. At the same time, venture capitalists realized that maybe, just maybe, growth wasn't the best metric after all. After all, what good is a billion-dollar valuation and $200 million in VC money if you're only generating $50 million in revenue? That's a recipe for disaster.

By 2022, this shift in attitudes began to have a clear impact on venture capital investment. While venture capital fundraising didn't slow down in terms of sheer dollars, the number of deals declined by 14 percent.[10] For over 250 days, not a single tech company had an IPO worth more than $50 million—the longest such period in the twenty-first century.[11] Investors were no longer falling over themselves to fund any startup with a promising idea. Before loosening their purse strings, they wanted to see that company's "path to profitability." In other words, they wanted to see evidence of a well-run business—evidence that many would-be unicorns were unable to provide.

To be clear, you can be a unicorn and still be a well-run business. You can even be a unicorn, be a well-run business, and experience massive contraction that's beyond your control (e.g., Zoom and Peloton). If you come by your unicorn status honestly and through a more-or-less balanced approach, then you've earned it—and you're well positioned for the long haul. But for far too many of these wannabe unicorns, their business strategy begins and ends with the dictum, "Grow at all costs."

That's a stupid strategy. Investors shouldn't offer money to companies unconcerned with building a quality, balanced busi-

---

10   Axios Pro, *What an Economic Downturn Means for VC, PE and M&A* (Axios, 2023), https://www.axios.com/pro/reports/economic-downturn-recession-vc-pe-manda.

11   Infinity Venture Capital, "Startups: Switching from High Growth to Profitability in 2022," October 12, 2022, https://infinityvc.net/startups-switching-from-high-growth-to-profitability-in-2022/.

ness, and companies shouldn't take that money if they're unsure whether they'll ever be able to repay it. Keep blindly following the herd, and you'll end up like the unicorns of mythology rather than the business world—extinct.

VALUATION IS NOT YOUR MOST IMPORTANT METRIC

In case you don't believe that pursuing balance plays in any economy, just look at one of the greatest unicorns of them all, Amazon. In an interview with *Bloomberg*, Amazon founder Jeff Bezos recalls a point near the peak of the internet bubble, around the turn of the century, when Amazon was trading for one hundred dollars a share. Of course, for those of us who remember, eventually that bubble burst, and that mighty Amazon stock tumbled all the way down to six dollars a share.

At the annual shareholder's meeting that year, Bezos started his presentation with one word: "Ouch."

As we all know, Amazon not only survived this moment, but grew to become one of the most successful companies in history. Why? Because while Amazon may have attained unicorn status, Bezos was focused on the fundamentals. As Bezos put it later, "The stock is not the company, and the company is not the stock."

Instead of prioritizing market share, Bezos focused on internal metrics—such as number of customers per profit unit. By these measures, "Every single thing about the business was getting better," Bezos said. "As the stock price was going the wrong way, everything inside the company was going the right way."

Was it harder to raise capital during this supposed tumble? Absolutely. But, as Bezos pointed out, Amazon already had all the money they needed to continue operating. And while the business wasn't profitable yet—something Wall Street continually punished them for—their gross margins were healthy and would eventually lead to a profitable company once they crossed a certain revenue threshold.[12]

Amazon understood a key component of the Unicorn Fallacy that so many investors and Wall Street analysts didn't: don't outgrow your capital. It's hard to stay in business when you run out of money. Focusing on metrics like gross margins, debt ratios, and customer retention allowed the company to be ready for a meteoric, healthy rise when the time was right. All investors and shareholders saw was a tanking valuation. If these myopically focused players had controlled Amazon's fate, it might have become another victim of the internet bubble. Patience and a lust for short-term profit, driven by valuation, don't often go well together.

But here's the problem: valuation isn't the most important metric of a successful business. In fact, it's not even in the top five. You can chase that billion-dollar valuation all you want, but if you haven't built a sustainable business focused on the key markers of success, then that valuation is meaningless. You have something that looks nice on paper but isn't real—a unicorn.

Valuation is not only an unhealthy pursuit; it's also often not real. The fall of the crypto empire is a good example—it can be totally made up or based on something as trivial as a news article. These "hot" companies are like winners of a popularity contest. For instance, Uber was almost a hectacorn after a decade of no profit and a mountain of debt.

The good news, though, is that the path to building a quality business is well worn. As leaders, we can swap out growth and valuation metrics for a quality metric and work to build a unicorn-proof organization. When you focus on building a

---

12   Jeff Bezos, "Jeff Bezos Says Amazon Stock Is 'Not the Company,'" Bloomberg Television, September 20, 2018, YouTube video, 2:51, https://www.youtube.com/watch?v=msFwJ5xpg_g.

quality business by targeting quality metrics, it won't matter whether the pendulum swings back toward growth at all costs a few years down the road. Instead of chasing the whims of the market, much like Amazon, you'll be positioning your organization for long-term success.

BALANCE WORKS IN ANY MARKET

In a growth-at-all-costs world, leaders focused on a popular SaaS metric known as the *rule of 40*. Determining your rule of 40 is simple. Just add your profit margin percentage (EBITDA) and your revenue growth percentage together. If those numbers total forty or higher, then you have an attractive company to investors.

WHAT ARE YOUR INTERNAL METRICS?

As we saw with the story of Amazon, valuation is an external measure that doesn't necessarily reflect the internal reality of your company. Revenue and revenue growth may be attractive external metrics, but if you get your internal metrics right, then you will build a quality business.

This begs the question: What *are* those internal metrics? Examples include:

- Bookings mix/sales mix
- Increases in installed base penetration
- Business win rates/close rates
- CAC/LTV

Measures like these speak to the fundamental *quality* of your business. Unfortunately, many aspiring unicorns either don't measure this data or don't pay much attention to the numbers. They're so concerned with revenue growth, they don't pay attention to other quality-focused metrics.

The rule of 40 applies to almost any business strategy. But just as important as reaching a healthy number is *how* you get there. When growth matters above all else, leaders are incentivized to take an unbalanced approach to hitting their rule of 40—often to the tune of 40 percent growth and 0 percent EBITDA.

The whole point of the rule is to balance growth and profit margins to reach forty or beyond. Tipping too far to one side or the other lands a company right back in unicorn territory which, in this new era, is not a good place to be if there isn't a strong foundation.

For a long time, Xactly followed an unbalanced approach to the rule of 40. You could see our priorities right in our tagline: "Incent right. Sell more." Our company's entire message was focused on quantity. We didn't care what you were selling—talent, tennis shoes, computers, airplanes, whatever. We were just going to help you sell more of it. If modern valuation metrics focused solely on growth, then we were going to sell our tools based on the *promise* of growth.

This approach worked...until it didn't.

After the market shifted in 2020, suddenly growth became a dirty word. Now, it was all about profitability, EBITDA, and real earnings. In other words, instead of worshipping growth—that is, on pure quantity of sales—today's leaders emphasize *quality* of sales. How do you build a company that can weather any economic environment?

By focusing on the balance inherent in any quality business.

The rule of 40 is a great metric when used properly, because building a balanced business has always been a good idea—even in the age of unicorns. Business trends are like any other. But the most successful companies in the long term don't chase trends. They focus on internal health. At the time of this writing, the pendulum has swung in favor of having a healthy EBITDA over a massive valuation. It stands to reason the pendulum might swing back in the other direction again one day.

Pursuing balance between growth and profit margins isn't a trend. EBITDA is the only thing that makes a business real when VC money and outside valuations get stripped away. It's essential in an economy focused on profitability. And it's a game changer/difference maker in a unicorn-crazy economy where so many bloated companies have nothing to stand on.

Our goal is to create a company that can withstand any economic conditions. The unbalanced approach works only in one very specific type of market, but balance can thrive in *any* market.

A balanced business is easier said than done. Growth has been ingrained in the minds of so many CEOs and leaders to the point where shifting strategies can seem insurmountable. So let's take the first step away from the old mentality right now.

WHAT DO YOU GET WHEN GROWTH IS ALL YOU'VE KNOWN?

For many leaders, the growth-at-all-costs model is all they've ever known.

Focusing on balance, on building a quality business, is a fundamentally different way of thinking—one that many business leaders I've spoken with aren't prepared for.

This brings me to my second point: prepare yourself. If you're accustomed to chasing the unicorn dream, then it's time to learn a new way of operating. A shift in focus to profitability has huge ramifications for your entire organization. It affects how you run your business, how you motivate your teams, how you think of your product mix, and how you pursue revenue.

Change, especially change of this magnitude, can be intimidating. If the risk of being left behind sounds a little doom and gloom, I don't mean it to be. There's risk in everything we do as business leaders, but that's never stopped us before. I don't focus on the risk in this instance, and neither should you. After all, the risk of doing nothing far outweighs the risk of trying and failing. What I see is a tremendous opportunity.

Many of the biggest and most successful companies in the world—those that have been in the game for a hundred years or more—have always understood the importance of building a balanced business. They run a playbook that incorporates steady growth and healthy profits, and they succeed by doing it better than their competitors. That strategy doesn't change when a flash-in-the-pan company comes along and grows until it explodes. Sustained success doesn't come from one decision, or by searching for a strategy that no one's ever thought of.

How often does a flash-in-the-pan even work out in the long run? Hardly ever, right? Success in this situation is about as rare as our proverbial unicorn. One of two things usually happens. One of the steady, balanced companies who've existed for decades acquires the hot company with unhealthy metrics. Or the former waits for the newcomer to end up in dire straits and then buys up the remnants—at a major discount. Either way, there's no alternative for steady success.

In a lot of ways, balance is the ultimate competitive edge—even if it's a foreign concept for all those companies who have gone all in on growth. But adapting to this new world is vital to survival. When profitability reigns as king in a mature market, the competitive edge becomes thinner and thinner. The difference between winners and losers shrinks.

Business and racing have this in common. In F1 racing, the top five cars often finish within a tenth of a second of each other. That's an incredibly narrow margin of error.

CASE STUDY: FLOWSERVE

Flowserve is a global manufacturer and service provider of fluid control devices operating in over fifty countries with over 17,500 employees worldwide. As a supplier of essential materials for innovative water-based projects around the world, Flowserve was a key player in the creation of the largest man-made river on Earth, as well as much-needed artificial snow production for the 2018 Winter Olympics.

In the months following the COVID-19 pandemic, the manufacturing industry was hit with a perfect storm of challenges, with interruptions to supply, demand, and workforce. For the first time in its 230-year history, Flowserve suddenly found itself encountering unprecedented challenges. They knew their customers, their products, and their organization, but they didn't know if they were being effective in day-to-day operations.

Xactly was able to build real-time visibility into Flowserve's global markets. What they discovered shocked them. Flowserve was underperforming, their funnel was elongating and moving away from buying decisions, quote volume and values were down, and conversion was low.

To combat this, Flowserve and Xactly focused on creating sales plans with actionable data insights, enabling their sales team to head into every sales conversation with a whole new set of tools at their disposal so they could get lead times down and more effectively drive customers through the sales funnel. They were also able to use Xactly's rich data insights to re-locate territories to reflect the rapidly changing economic landscape.

These insights simply weren't possible when Flowserve was working off of spreadsheets (see Chapter 4). With Xactly's suite, Lowe was able to design enterprise incentive compensation plans and drive behaviors around a narrow set of key objectives. Further, through the use of dashboards, they're able to track their performance in real time. If something looks off, they're able to immediately drill down to understand the potential problem areas.

In some ways, these may sound like small changes to the company's sales processes. However, as Lowe would attest, these changes have been vital in keeping Flowserve functioning and stable in a time of great economic uncertainty.

To F1 teams, winning isn't about finding some massive modification that will blow all the other cars off the track. It's about gaining the most minute edge, the most minute advantage.

Of course, in business, we don't have to worry about beating out the competition by a tenth of a second. However, many leaders often make the mistake of taking extreme measures just to hit 25 percent profitability overnight, for instance.

That doesn't work—and thinking like that can often do more harm than good. Instead, do what the F1 teams do. Focus on small, incremental improvements that will add up over time and drive your business toward better results. Look for anything that can provide even a small advantage, and then pursue it relentlessly. *That's* how you create a more balanced rule of 40.

INTELLIGENT REVENUE TUNE-UP

→ How focused is your company on growth? Do you find yourself sacrificing profitability for growth?

→ How does your business stack up against the rule of 40? If you do hit 40, how balanced is your approach?

→ What are your metrics of success?

→ Do you see any red flags that you might not be producing quality revenue?

CHAPTER 2

INTRODUCING INTELLIGENT REVENUE

THERE WAS A TIME WHEN SAAS WAS NEW.

Not only was it new, it was mind-boggling. Software as a service? What does that even mean? What do you mean it's in the cloud? What is this cloud, and where is it? How does it function?

This was the landscape when Xactly first hit the scene in 2005. To get B2B customers to buy our service, it was clear we had a lot of explaining to do. We were SaaS pioneers and slowly, companies began buying into our respective platforms and understanding how we worked. Many questions still persisted, but at least customers were getting on board. Just like that, we were gaining momentum and feeling good about our future.

Two years later, I got a call from our head of sales: we were about to lose all of our customers.

Not because we'd done something wrong. We hadn't. But their contracts were about to expire. We had to resell them on the merits of our product—and then again a year or two later, and again a year or two after that.

This was easier said than done. Clients pointed out bugs in the system, features they wanted to see, and design issues they didn't like—all to try to get a better deal on the service. We welcomed any feedback on our product, of course, but in the meantime, we needed stable, predictable revenue to deliver those upgrades. If we could entice customers into longer contracts—say, three to five years at a minimum—they would see that the product they had bought into was constantly improving.

The question was, how?

For a wannabe unicorn, that solution is simple, although not necessarily sustainable: throw your sales team at the problem. Incentivize them to make whatever deals they can—renewals, new business, poached business, it doesn't matter. Just get that revenue in the door, even if it means offering steep discounts. As long as they sell more volume, the growth-at-all-costs makes sense, they'll be able to solve any of their business's money-related problems.

An Intelligent Revenue perspective says otherwise. Sales volume can be a good thing, but more important is the quality of revenue you're bringing in.

In the last chapter, we debunked the Unicorn Fallacy and established the importance of balancing growth and profits. In this chapter, we'll zoom in on the driver of any quality business: your revenue operation. With an Intelligent Revenue framework, you will be able to build a revenue engine not only fine-tuned for growth, but for *quality* of revenue.

More than that, you will have an organization built for the future. Recent innovations like generative artificial intelligence (AI) are revolutionizing best practices in every organization in every industry. Overall, I see this as a win-win for both organization and employee. After all, who wouldn't want a highly adaptive and insightful copilot to help them get their work done?

We'll explore this bright new future in Chapter 10. To get there, let's start at the beginning with an exploration of what Intelligent Revenue is and why this approach is so essential to the long-term health of your organization.

ALL REVENUE IS NOT CREATED EQUAL

Does your sales compensation plan factor in metrics like length of contract and annual increases?

Are you thinking about bookings, retention, EBITDA?

Usually, when I ask a company's leadership team these questions, I get one of two responses.

The first camp—the bigger camp—says, "Nah, we don't really care."

The second says, "We care a lot about those metrics, but we don't know how to do that."

The former camp may be wrong, but at least they're honest. Each camp may have different priorities, but they're both leaving a tremendous opportunity on the table—all because they're too preoccupied with day-to-day operations to do anything about it.

Here's an example to illustrate this point. Imagine two sales reps who have each just closed similar $100,000 SaaS deals.

- Deal 1: a one-year contract for $100,000, with no increases
- Deal 2: a five-year $100,000 contract with annual increases and a mix of products that include some of your organization's more profitable offerings

Which deal is better for your company?

The latter deal, obviously. Not only does it represent much smarter revenue, but it locks the client in for a longer term—creating more stable and predictable revenue for your organization. Plus, it focuses on a more profitable product mix.

But here's an important question: Does your company incentivize its reps to prioritize the second deal over the first deal?

If you're like most companies, probably not. It's possible you pay out more to your sales reps for multiyear deals, but few to none of you incentivize the annual increases—a surefire way to grow your revenue year over year. If you found a way to do that, wouldn't your business be more successful?

This is what Intelligent Revenue is all about: prioritizing strategies that change the composition of your revenue. While most organizations lack the systems or infrastructure to differentiate between these two deals, organizations that follow an Intelligent Revenue approach can proactively identify those differences—incentivizing the higher-value deals throughout the entire revenue operation.

Now, extrapolate those differences beyond two deals from two reps and consider their impact on all your deals. What would the net effect have on your business, especially in times of economic uncertainty?

An easy example is the massive disruptions caused by the COVID-19 pandemic in 2020. For the organizations that weathered these disruptions well—and in many cases, thrived—their leadership focused on a few essential questions:

- Can our business weather downturns?
- Can we weather shocks from market forces, politics, and disruptors?
- Is leadership prioritizing a sustainable revenue model?

Some organizations realized they weren't in good shape and pivoted to make their business model more nimble and resilient. Others realized they had a solid foundation and worked to accentuate their strengths. In either case, the focus shifted from simply obtaining revenue to creating revenue velocity—that is, earning revenue at a sustainable rate and with the greatest long-term benefit to the organization.

A shift to revenue velocity has benefited these companies in the post-COVID world, as more companies embrace a shift to remote work and cloud-based workspaces. That sounds great on the surface, but success in a new business landscape isn't a license to revert back to chasing unicorn status. With opportunity comes competition, and subscription exhaustion—not to mention standing out in a saturated market—has made the SaaS landscape more cutthroat than ever. This industry has seen revenue growth, but remaining focused on the right *type* of revenue growth remains vital.[13]

As I said in the Introduction, Intelligent Revenue is about building sustainable, predictable, resilient revenue models adaptive to any market force—even a pandemic. It's not about operating more opportunistically, but about building a unified, de-siloed revenue operation built for the long haul.

One essential component of Intelligent Revenue is tracking progress toward desired outcomes. However, all the data in the world is only as good as the objectives that drive it. How will you go to market? What behaviors will you incentivize? How can you ensure accurate forecasts? How will you embrace AI and use data to improve sales performance? Can your sales leaders call their numbers with conviction? How you answer these

13 Paddle, "The State of SaaS 2022: A Meta Report," accessed April 29, 2023, https://www.paddle.com/resources/state-of-saas-meta-report.

questions will help you make critical choices as you embrace an Intelligent Revenue system.

HOW TO TARGET QUALITY OVER QUANTITY

Before you can begin to apply the fundamental principles of Intelligent Revenue to your business, it's imperative to understand how a quality-over-quantity mindset works on a large scale. Here are the core principles underpinning any Intelligent Revenue–based initiative.

PRIORITIZE DIVERSE REVENUE STREAMS

An Intelligent Revenue approach prioritizes diversity on multiple levels using data-driven insights to weather downturns or shocks from market forces, political forces, or other disruptions and gain a competitive edge. Remember, as we all weather each new storm from our respective boats, we all experience external shocks differently. A vertical-specific company and a broader, horizontal company (such as Xactly) will have very different experiences in the same market conditions.

For example, during the height of the COVID-19 pandemic, we found that our retail customers suffered from considerable contraction, while some of our tech customers did very well. As a horizontal company involved in many industries, Xactly was well positioned to weather this fluctuation. Other, more vertical companies focused solely on retail, for instance, didn't fare nearly as well. They lived or died based on their business model. In this instance, prioritizing diversity was a hell of a lot better than crossing our fingers and hoping our industry wouldn't be affected.

While this is just one small example, there are many ways that diverse revenue streams can help a business:

1. **Diversity of products.** Growing multiple products provides companies with multiple revenue streams, allowing them to weather changes in the market, customer preferences, business cycles, etc.
2. **Diversity of geographies.** Economic conditions can vary among geographic locations. A diverse set of markets allows companies to deliver steadier revenues as they can compensate for down markets with up markets.
3. **Diversity of partners.** Companies should build ecosystems filled with different kinds of partners. In our case, this is other software providers, systems integrators, or resellers. Our partnerships range from large global companies to smaller, regional companies. Partner diversification enables us to cover the market more effectively.
4. **Diversity of employees.** This may be a stretch in this context, but having a diverse group of employees allows us to reduce the downsides of groupthink and echo chambers. In turn, we are able to see opportunities more quickly.

Diversity in all forms only serves to strengthen a business. Think back to the unicorn company. It can only do one thing—grow. A quality business has to be good at many things and must have a sustainable revenue foundation that can survive changing market conditions. Of course, as you'll see in the next section, there is more than one way to do this.

CREATE TRIBUTARIES

In our experience, we've learned that there is more than one way to prepare an egg—that is, there isn't just one way to pursue quality revenue in your organization, but several—what we at Xactly like to call *tributaries*.

The larger your organization, the larger and more sophisticated your sales operation. Within these operations, given the sheer volume of dollars and reps in play, even small changes make a big difference.

Let me explain what I mean. Earlier in the chapter, I asked you to consider whether you'd prefer (1) a one-year contract for $100,000, with no increases, or (2) a five-year, $100,000 contract with annual increases and a mix of products that include some of your organization's more profitable offerings. The latter will always be better for your business, but that doesn't mean that every single contract that comes in needs to look exactly like it. Other quality-focused approaches could work equally as well:

- Improving annual rate increases between 1 to 5 percent
- Improving your churn rate by prioritizing five-year deals over one-year deals
- Incentivizing higher-margin products

Any of these targets would not only be more practical, but would also make a positive contribution to your overall revenue velocity. If you're a billion-dollar business, what would those changes be worth? How many more customers would you retain each year?

Naturally, these particular goals might not apply to the needs of your organization. In all the organizations I've spoken with over the years, I've never heard the same set of tributaries twice.

Ultimately, it's up to you to set the goals. You drive the change; Intelligent Revenue is merely the rudder.

The point is, when you're focused on revenue quality, it's not about the one path to revenue. It's about all paths. Alone, each of these approaches has value. Together, your tributaries add up to major shifts in revenue, forming a gushing river of positive impact. No one change solves all your problems. However, by increasing the number of good ideas and improvements, you improve the quality of deals.

When you conduct little experiments, you might find certain approaches aren't helpful or don't apply. The beauty of an Intelligent Revenue approach is that you don't have to wait until the next quarter or the next fiscal year to change course. When utilized properly, a tributary-focused approach provides you with feedback in real time.

GENERATE DATA-DRIVEN INSIGHTS

A very long time ago—nearly two decades ago as I write this book—someone at our fledgling company had the bright idea to include in our contracts that we had the right to aggregate and anonymize our customers' data.

This wasn't typical contractual language at the time. But, as one of the earliest entries into the SaaS game, we were accustomed to making our own rules, and we thought that control of our data might come in handy down the line. We had no idea how important that data would become, and we also had no idea how willing our customers would be to share their data. In fact, I was certain that our customers *wouldn't* agree to it. Still, we added the clause to our contracts anyway, thinking that even if 30 percent of our customers *did* agree to share their data, that would give us a pretty statistically relevant sample set.

All these years later, I'm proud to report that 97 percent of our customers opt into our data-sharing program. The dataset we've collected represents billions of annual transactions. Add those billions up year over year for nearly twenty years, and we've ended up with an incredible treasure trove of usable data that has become the core element driving all our products.

Here, I want to be absolutely clear, since I don't want to be misunderstood as another "data for the sake of data" peddler.

Data is great. But data without intelligence is meaningless.

I have zero patience listening to pitches from companies that mindlessly go on and on about data, data, data. It's nauseating. Everybody talks about data, but no one seems to know what it means. And when pressed to get specific, they highlight types of data that aren't especially meaningful to me or the leaders I work with.

Don't fall for those pitches. Data for data's sake is meaningless. Focus instead on what the data should get you: intelligence. Challenge the people you're working with to give you insights and actionable takeaways, such as:

- How is your company performing?
- Have your sales reps performed against their goals?
- How does your performance stack up against the best in class?

As we like to say at Xactly: show me, tell me, coach me. Show me the relevant data, explain to me what it means and why it's important, and coach me on how to use that knowledge to improve performance. We use our deep datasets to drive actionable insights into our revenue operation—improving our ability to predict what deals will close and what deals are in danger, to coach and incentivize our sales reps around the behaviors we want, and to dramatically improve forecasting so that we can plan expenses around our business with confidence.

These insights come together to paint the picture of our business. Put another way, they tell the story of where we've been in the market, where we are, and where we're headed.

FIND THE STORY

Like so much in the business world, data-driven processes evolved as a result of two things: (1) trial and error, and (2) customer demand.

What was driving that customer demand? The *story*. To flip Simon Sinek's oft-quoted statement on its head, businesses don't just want to know what their customers are doing. They want to know *why* they're doing it. Eventually, many SaaS providers (ourselves included), realized that we had the data that could tell those stories—all we had to do was package it in a useful way.

No matter their industry, these data-based stories have the ability to save organizations unimaginable amounts of time. To explain how, let me give you an easy example.

Imagine that you're Amazon. On every single product page, you offer a list of suggestions. These suggestions tell a story. For instance, customers who viewed or bought this item also bought these other products. That's an incredibly useful insight—both for the retailer and the consumer. By making these connections, Amazon is able to better understand the customer profiles for certain products. On the flip side of the coin, seeing these suggestions provides Amazon customers with more information on other products they might need in addition to the ones they're viewing.

Story-driven insights like these are incredibly useful. No doubt, you've purchased an extra product or two through

Amazon as a result of this feature—powered entirely by data mining and AI. All Amazon has to do is leverage the buyer data they collect with every purchase, filter it through its algorithm, and *voilà!* Instant value.

The alternative—a manual approach to these same insights—simply wouldn't be worth it. Imagine if, for every single product page, you had a dedicated employee sort through purchase data and determine the other most commonly purchased or viewed items. Oh, and you had to update this information constantly. On a spreadsheet.

If that doesn't sound ridiculous, it at least sounds exhausting.

And yet, every time a sales leader sits down at a spreadsheet to churn out their annual go-to-market or sales compensation plan, that's exactly what they're doing. Sure, they're pulling from the previous year or quarter's data, but it's still a manual operation that takes a lot of time and is prone to human error. And of course, the data they're drawing from is based only on their company's performance.

Imagine how much time it might save if you could stand on the shoulders of giants—years and years and years of data from folks who have sat in your chair in similar situations. Not only would you have greater insight into where you need to go, but also into what obstacles to look out for along the way.

Unfortunately, most businesses don't have a revenue operation powered by this type of automated intelligence. Beyond sheer exhaustion, there are inherent problems with the traditional approach that must be acknowledged so we can plot a better path forward.

CASE STUDY: IFS

IFS is a large, four thousand–person enterprise software company based in Europe, with about six hundred salespeople in total. When they first began working with Xactly, IFS was in the midst of a three-year transformation journey to consolidate its nine on-premises ERP solutions, relocate them to the cloud, and replace its forecasting system with a tool that could scale rapidly along with the company.

This was no small effort. Prior to their transformation journey, IFS's entire revenue operation was decentralized. Everyone approached their responsibilities in their own way, with no internal consistency, even among team members in similar roles. Reps in one place had very different processes from reps in other places.

To complicate matters, IFS's initial attempts to centralize systems and processes had taken them in the wrong direction. Initially, they attempted to build their own forecasting tool on top of another provider's analytics product. This presented several problems. The tool's functions were limited to forecasting, the tool itself was limited to fewer functions than they had envisioned, and, just to add insult to injury, it took forever to update.

Looking for a better solution, IFS partnered with Xactly to build an enterprise platform that could de-silo their sales operation, connect them as a global company, and most importantly, forecast with confidence and accuracy. We were able to help them do precisely that, centralizing quota and territory planning, performance incentives, and forecasting. As a result, they were able to integrate across the various branches of their company and use data-driven insights to plan and predict with much more certainty.

The result has been a game changer. Since implementing their enterprise system, IFS has increased sales productivity by 10 to 15 percent, improved CRM accuracy by 20 to 30 percent, and restored trust between the company's sales leaders and the C-suite. Today, as Grant Blenkinsopp, IFS's Director of Business Operations, says, "I can attend a call without having my heart in my throat. I know the sales forecasting data will be available and accurate at critical moments."

THE RULE OF X: INTELLIGENT REVENUE IN ACTION

Now that you understand the core principles behind an Intelligent Revenue mindset, let's put those into practice with a practice known as the Rule of X.

For the first few years of its existence, Xactly's tagline was, "Incent right. Sell more." Like most organizations, we employed a patchwork strategy for revenue growth that amounted to a bunch of semi-informed stabs in the dark.

From a sales perspective, those stabs went something like this: A sales rep signs a company to a one-year deal. From their perspective, it's easier to do, the payout is usually the same as a multiyear deal, and they can raise rates during renewal time. On the other hand, it's generally assumed that buyers want to avoid getting locked into a multiyear contract—unless they also get to lock in their rate. This assumption is half-true, but we'll get to that in a second.

Overall, this approach lands companies in something of a sales bind. Every year, they have to raise prices. And every year, their sales reps have to return to the same accounts, explain the price increase, and justify why there's still value. Sure, if the product is good, a lot of those buyers *will* re-sign. But as anyone in the SaaS world can tell you, churn is real. Constant renewals give customers too many chances to jump ship.

PROPOSING A NEW SOLUTION

The Rule of X ties into our emphasis on diversification. The solution isn't one giant change but rather a thousand little tributaries that eventually converge. To grow an organization, any one change isn't dramatic—but the combination of twenty or thirty smaller initiatives can be transformational. Pennies and dimes add up to real dollars. Soon, instead of 20 percent growth, you're sitting at 24 percent—a tremendous difference over time.

The Rule of X isn't *the* solution by itself, but combined with other tributaries, it has the potential to make a big impact.

At the Rule of X's core is a simple question: What if the goal were to target five-year deals with 5 percent annual increases? The breakdown on a deal starting at $100,000 might look like this:

- Year 1: $100,000
- Year 2: $105,000
- Year 3: $110,250
- Year 4: $115,762.50
- Year 5: $121,550.63

By the contract's end, you're earning over $20,000 more on the deal than when you began. Compare that to the traditional approach, where one of two things happens: the client locks in the same rate for the duration of the contract, or you risk losing them every year when it comes time to renegotiate. Instead, you have a guaranteed increase in revenue for each year of the contract's life. Multiply this increase across a customer base of a thousand or more, and the Rule of X is a game changer.

Of course, if you're like me, you're skeptical any customer would agree to something like this. The very idea was hard for me to get my mind around. I'd been in the sales trenches for years, and my gut screamed that this was a suicide mission.

Luckily, my peers didn't listen to me.

ENACTING THE RULE OF X

Now that you understand the Rule of X's basic goal, let's discuss how to drive behavior.

The "X" in the Rule of X is based on the Roman numeral for ten. The goal, in effect, is to get the contract's term and yearly rate increase to equal ten. For instance, a five-year increase at 5 percent each year equals ten. (5 years + 5 percent = 10)

That's the ideal outcome, but it's not the only outcome. The exact deal depends on what the rep and the customer agree to and how much the increase is per year. For example:

- A four-year deal with a 4 percent ARR = Rule of 8
- A five-year deal with a 3 percent ARR = Rule of 8
- A three-year deal with a 3 percent ARR = Rule of 6
- A two-year deal with a 1 percent ARR = Rule of 3

Any of these outcomes is more beneficial than a basic one-year deal. To incentivize a Rule of X outcome, we set the Rule of 6 as neutral—in our case, a 5 percent commission. We didn't care if reps sold a three-year deal with a 3 percent ARR or a five-year deal with a 1 percent ARR; we just cared that they met the threshold. If they landed a hundred-thousand-dollar contract, they netted five thousand dollars.

Now, here's where the Rule of X acts as a commission modifier. For every Rule of X the rep went up, they got a higher percentage of commission:

- Rule of 7 = 6 percent commission
- Rule of 8 = 7 percent commission
- Rule of 9 = 8 percent commission
- Rule of X = 9 percent commission

As you can see, at almost double the baseline, a Rule of X is the kind of incentive that gets people's attention. Like all incentivization programs, this approach amounts to nothing more than a carrot and a stick—but this carrot is incredibly enticing.

Of course, the carrot works the other way too. The way we structured our Rule of X program, if a sales rep only hit a Rule of 5, their commission dropped to 3 percent. Did we still get some deals below a Rule of 6? Sure, but reps only closed those deals when they absolutely had to—say, for an exceptionally large deal with a high enough overall commission to absorb the hit.

THE RESULTS SPEAK FOR THEMSELVES

I was flabbergasted at the average contracts after our first year of implementing the Rule of X.

Initially, our average contracts were twenty-two months with no annual increases. Like so many organizations, we relied on securing an increase at renewal. In the first year that we instituted this modifier, though, our *average* new deal was a Rule of 8—buoyed by a staggering amount of Rule of X deals.

Not only was I wrong, I was *really* wrong.

At the time, I didn't fully appreciate the tributary approach. I got the idea, but I didn't think so many tiny streams could converge into an unstoppable force. In reality, I shouldn't have been so surprised by the benefits:

- **Pure quality measurement.** Previously, reps closed one-year deals without annual increases because the term was twelve months. When they signed multiyear deals, they catered to customers' appreciation of locked-in pricing.
- **Fewer off-ramps.** The Rule of X signs customers to a five-year deal, with no exit during that time period. There are

fewer opportunities for the customer to quit, naturally improving churn rates.

- **Less time at the negotiating table.** Signing long-term contracts with customers shifts the focus to attracting new business and retaining clients, rather than renegotiating year after year.
- **Greater value to the customer.** At first, customers might bristle at the idea of a 5 percent annual increase. In reality, they face a higher rate hike when they try to renew yearly. When faced with the choice between a fixed 5 percent yearly increase and a variable hike of 9 percent or more, most would choose the former.
- **Built-in yearly increases for the majority of the customer base.** A SaaS company with $200 million in revenue and built-in 4 percent step-ups sees $8 million in annual revenue increases. That's four points of guaranteed growth before we get out of bed to find new customers.

Just like that, we targeted 24 percent yearly growth over the usual 20 percent. Extrapolated, that shift became hundreds of millions of additional revenue dollars—all because we focused on quality of revenue and successfully incentivized that focus.

CEOs with long-term success recognize that what got you *here* won't get you *there*. If I'd stuck with what I'd known, I never would have been willing to try—much less embrace—the Rule of X. But once I understood the principle was designed to target quality of revenue, drive the right behaviors, and make outcomes predictable, I became its biggest champion.

The Rule of X is just one example of how an Intelligent Revenue approach can transform your business. But once you realize a better method isn't only possible but also attainable, why wouldn't you change your approach? "Sell more" may have worked for Xactly at one point, but now we sell smarter by incentivizing long-term contracts with annual increases.

WHERE DO YOU WANT TO GO FROM HERE?

Many years ago, Brian Solis, the global innovation evangelist at Salesforce, popularized the concept of *digital Darwinism*. According to Solis, people who failed to survive the age of digital transformation would not necessarily be ineffective or worse in their offerings. They'd simply be too slow. In this new paradigm, it's not enough to be the smartest. You also have to be the fastest, which requires up-to-the-minute information that enables you to pivot in a new direction.

An Intelligent Revenue approach allows you to do both—be the smartest and the fastest. But to realize its benefits, you have to throw your hat in the ring. And to do that, first you must accept that "we've always done it this way" won't cut it anymore. Outdated thinking will keep you mired in the Stone Age.

- A conventional go-to-market plan might work, but there's always room for it to be more effective. In a business world where speed is vital, Intelligent Revenue creates a sales plan faster.
- A company without Intelligent Revenue might generate a healthy amount of revenue, but it could be better. Quality businesses not only hit revenue goals, but they more accurately predict outcomes.
- Your system might not seem broken, even if it is, but it could be faster. Why waste time on tasks like processing commissions that could (and should) be automated?
- Even the best sales leader has room to become more accurate. There's simply too much data to process and convert to

usable insights without assistance. An Intelligent Revenue business increases that prized accuracy.

Boosts in productivity and accuracy can have incredible benefits for your bottom line. That matters. But it's only half the story. Behind these numbers lies the human experience of your team members, from senior leadership to finance to sales reps.

Intelligent Revenue has the potential to guide marked improvements in so-called soft metrics like behaviors, relationships, and transparency. These factors kill productivity when they're not being met—and can turbocharge your results when they are.

After all, forecasting at nearly 100 percent accuracy is nice, but how you're treated as a result matters more. Instead of going into every quarter holding your breath and crossing your fingers, you can hold your head high knowing that you'll likely hit the target.

Suddenly, all those *what went wrong?* conversations disappear. The more time you can save by not having to dissect every mistake, the more time you can spend improving your business. A more holistic understanding of the state of their revenue operation better positions sales leaders to develop more predictive plans and focused targets. As a result, they can go from struggling in the middle to leading the pack.

The question is, how do you systematize the Intelligent Revenue process? In the next few chapters, we'll explore how to apply an Intelligent Revenue approach in each of the major functions of your revenue operation—Planning, Performing, and Predicting.

INTELLIGENT REVENUE TUNE-UPS

→ How strong is your revenue engine's diversity? Do you have enough tributaries?

→ How frequently does your company use data-driven insights to gain a competitive edge?

→ What's stopping your company from implementing the Rule of X? Would your sales team embrace this change?

CHAPTER 3

PREPARE FOR CHANGE

IN THE BOOK *THE HUNDREDTH MONKEY*, AUTHOR KEN Keyes, Jr. tells the story of a group of monkeys living together on an island and trying to learn how to use a particular tool. The first ninety-nine monkeys can't figure the tool out. Then the hundredth monkey comes along and unlocks the secret. Soon, as a result of this monkey's breakthrough, *all* the monkeys on the island know how to use the tool too.

So what's this have to do with you? I'm not seriously comparing you to a bunch of monkeys on an island, am I?

Yes, I am—but there's a point. I promise.

Like the monkeys, many of the people we work with on Intelligent Revenue solutions have similar problems, even if they describe those problems in different ways. Our job has been listening to all these sales leaders from different companies describe their problems and to begin to extract the common threads.

Once we identify the right pattern, we create a solution. And once we create that solution, everyone else we work with knows how to do what we know how to do.

Of course, getting there takes a big leap. Up to this point, you've been a spreadsheet monkey, operating on an old, mundane, and time-consuming manual system with little to show for it except for some basic, error-riddled intelligence (more on that in Chapter 4). The old way is what you know, but it's not exactly helping your career or adding value to the company.

Now, you have a chance to be an Intelligent Revenue thought leader. To adapt an approach and tool set that frees you up to think more strategically about your company. To become an internal thought leader. To replan and re-optimize your revenue operation. To be the hundredth monkey in the room.

This isn't a painless switch. Like any digital transformation effort, bringing Intelligent Revenue to your organization means adopting a new system and set of tools. To do this correctly, you need the support of both leadership and internal stakeholders—which means convincing them that a solution better than a spreadsheet exists and then persuading them to prioritize a switch. After that, you need to learn how these new tools work and then train everyone in your revenue operation on how to use them too.

If that sounds like a lot, it is. The payoff, however, is a revenue operation focused on quality of revenue with its sales leaders free to think strategically about how to drive results.

To harness the IR approach, you must first understand your current business, including your talent needs, your leadership needs, and which parts of the business need to evolve. The transformation isn't massive, but it also isn't entirely localized, touching stakeholders in finance, sales, operations, sales leadership, and other business areas. In working on adoption, it's important to get all those people singing from the same hymnal so you can move together in unison. That's exactly what this chapter aims to accomplish.

STARTING YOUR INTELLIGENT REVENUE JOURNEY

Before you can sync the various branches of your organization with this new paradigm, you must gain a better understanding of where you lie on the Intelligent Revenue curve. Knowing your starting point dictates what will follow. How prepared are you to take your revenue operation to the next level?

Maybe you're unsure of your company's preparedness. Don't worry, I have a solution. Xactly's Maturity Model can help you determine the health of your revenue operation and design your Intelligent Revenue journey. It offers insight into where you are right now—and where your strengths and weaknesses lie—to better equip you to realign your revenue operation around an Intelligent Revenue model.

Understanding your current state allows you to paint a picture of your future state based on your unique business goals. Maybe you want to be more disciplined in your planning. Maybe you want to do a better job connecting your incentive schemes to actual corporate goals. Whatever the case, once you know where you are and where you want to go, the Maturity Model builds out the in-between steps to help you get there.

THE MATURITY MODEL

How reliable are your go-to-market strategies? Are you incentivizing the behaviors that you want to drive, or are your sales reps going rogue? Are your sales forecasts reasonably close to reality, or do you see opportunities for improvement? Using the Maturity Model as your starting point, let's find out.

LEVEL 1: GROUND FLOOR

This is where 85 percent of all the eventual IR adopters we work with start out. You have an all-manual revenue operation that's dependent on spreadsheets. Because of the manual nature of your system, you have few, if any, repeatable revenue and performance processes. Any tech you use is either ad hoc or homegrown.

In other words, you aren't relying on the tools at your disposal. When you're right, it's usually because you got lucky rather than because the data led you there. Nothing is repeatable, and your leaders spend too much time keeping the ship afloat rather than contemplating the bigger picture.

If you're at this level, your top priority is to get started and get comfortable. In Part 2 of the book, focus your energy on Chapters 4 and 5. Embracing a few modern tools and restructuring your compensation plan to align with an Intelligent Revenue mindset are vital pieces of the foundation we're building. Those moves alone will help to improve your revenue operation by leaps and bounds.

LEVEL 2: SOME BASIC AUTOMATION

At this level, you've already begun automating certain processes in your revenue operation, moving on from the hellscape of spreadsheets and migrating into some automated software.

To give an example of what this looks like from a practical standpoint, at level 2, your sales reps would no longer receive their comp plans as a Word doc. Instead, they would receive their plans through software that automates the whole process based on your inputs. Then, once the rep agrees to the plan, they would use a DocuSign feature instead of emailing it back. Automation allows for full reporting on who has signed and who hasn't in real time.

This is just one example of adding a tool to remove the manual burden from your system. From here, your top priority is to reevaluate the culture of your revenue operation—particularly your sales team. Chapters 4 and 5 will still be valuable to you, but Chapters 6 and 7 will help take your effort to the next level.

LEVEL 3: INTEGRATION

Very few companies step into the Maturity Model at the integration stage. That would require dedication to automating certain business practices, and, more importantly, a thorough understanding of how areas of the operation can work in concert and even steer one another.

What do we mean by that? In level 2, as you began to automate, you also began collecting data. That's the real beauty of software-mediated business processes: their ability to capture all the information.

Next, think about how you can use this data to begin integrating your business processes. Ideally, the planning function shares data with the comp function, the comp function shares data with the forecasting function, the forecasting function feeds back into the planning function, and so on. Because they share their data, each of these systems is now self-reinforcing—it keeps getting better based on feedback from the other systems.

The very idea of this kind of integration in a spreadsheet is nonexistent. How would you even begin to sync your go-to-market strategy with your compensation? Someone would have to manually compare the two documents and carry over the relevant data.

By level 3, you've mastered the basics. Now, it's time to learn how to use all your newfound revenue intelligence to diversify your sales approach, drive target behaviors, and watch your operation grow in a way that can be accurately forecasted. Chapters 8 and 9 will show you how to do it.

LEVEL 4: OPTIMIZATION

As you can imagine, no one starts at level 4. Think of this more as an end state after you have built a mature Intelligent Revenue operation.

By this point, the facets of your operation are running smoothly and piggybacking off one another in real time. You're living by the mantra that data is power when it can be digested and used in a way that lends a competitive edge. Major decisions and long-term strategy still fall to your company's leaders, but much of the day-to-day processes rely upon automation tools. Optimization pulls your people out of the weeds so they can focus on the bigger picture.

This is also where all the fun happens. If you have built out a fully automated and integrated system, you'd be well positioned to begin driving tremendous insights through all the data you've collected, aggregated, and integrated into the platform. What is the data telling you? What are the key insights? What are the key predictions? What recommendations can you make? More importantly, what's next? In Chapter 10, we'll explore the future of Intelligent Revenue and how AI will be a key driver in that process.

We already stressed that the Maturity Model will help you get from start to finish on your Intelligent Revenue journey. But every company's path is unique. What does your ultimate objective look like? Where do you see yourself when this is all said and done?

BEGIN WITH THE END IN MIND

What does Intelligent Revenue look like to you? What are the end goals for your business that this framework would enable?

The most successful Intelligent Revenue organizations begin with the end in mind because it's the most efficient way to get to where you're trying to go. Is your goal expansion? Increased market share? A new customer base? All of the above? Whatever the case, by clearly stating your end goals and then working backward to determine how to achieve them, you will develop a plan that incorporates all the different intersection points along the value chain to drive the kind of behaviors we have discussed throughout this book.

This is an inherently proactive approach, skating to where the puck will be, not where it is now. Instead of reactively trying to solve the problems at hand, you're focused on adopting solutions that will bring you long-term success.

To be proactive rather than reactive, first you need to answer the following basic questions about your business, the challenges it faces, and the people who will help bring about change.

#1: WHAT ARE YOUR TALENT NEEDS?

A digital transformation isn't as simple as a snap of your fingers. Whatever new path you choose to pursue, it needs to be implemented by real people within the organization. These are the people who are going to get into the nitty-gritty work necessary to make this transformation happen—and then ensure that the intersection points between, for example, finance and your sales team integrate seamlessly.

To do this, you will need to either reassign some team members to take on new roles and responsibilities or hire new team members capable of driving your transformation. In either case, to make sure you're recruiting the right people, your first priority is gaining clarity on the skills, experience, and capabilities needed. This is not the time for offering stretch opportunities. Identify people who already know how to do the work and who can execute in a high-level, orderly way.

Similarly, it's also important that your talent—new or existing—is aligned with the goals and value of your Intelligent Revenue initiative. Here is a brief look at the stakeholders who absolutely need to be bought in:

- **Finance.** In general, the finance team members who manage your current manual systems absolutely need to be involved, from the finance ops and comp managers, all the way up to the VP of finance and the CFO. Involving the finance department lets them know from day one that incorporating IR frees them up to be even more critical to the company's financial health—and that building a strong revenue operation isn't purely in the hands of sales.
- **Sales Generation.** This group isn't the primary driver of a switch to Intelligent Revenue, but they are the end users, which means they wield tremendous influence in terms of a successful adoption. As such, it's important to have them weigh in on the comp side—if only to the extent that they can confirm their current system needs improvement and an overhaul would boost morale and productivity.
- **IT.** Remember, part of Intelligent Revenue's competitive advantage is data-dependent. Your IT team has access to all your company's data, both the data required to run your manual system and other data that may ultimately prove valuable. Without their buy-in, good luck connecting the many disparate data sources in a useful way that will drive insights.

- **HR.** Human resources is like the glue that holds your workforce together. They should be leaned upon during any major change, especially a transition to Intelligent Revenue. Your company needs HR now more than ever, for messaging, helping track and optimize shifting roles, onboarding the right talent, and managing expectations throughout the process.

Each of these groups has a part to play. However, it's important that roles and decision-making are clearly delineated. If you try to take a fully consensus-driven approach, you'll probably never make a decision. Instead, designate a smaller group to make the important decisions, while ensuring there are appropriate systems to solicit and consider feedback.

Why is this so important? Because organizations are diverse places. Everyone thinks in a slightly different way. You could state a plan to a room full of twenty people, and each one of them could walk out with their own interpretation of the plan's execution. Differing perspectives are useful, but they can't be a barrier to action.

It's for this reason that strategic alignment is so critical—and that you recognize the scope of the lift you're asking everyone to undertake. If you've been driving your revenue operation with spreadsheets and gut instinct, a switch to an Intelligent Revenue system represents a large pivot for the whole organization, specific business areas, and individuals within those areas. It's no small feat, but it can revolutionize how you do business. To reach the finish line, you have to put into it what you want to get out. This starts from the top down.

#2: WHAT ARE YOUR LEADERSHIP NEEDS?

Not everyone is going to think about adopting an Intelligent Revenue framework in the same way. From the CFO to the VP of sales to the rank-and-file team members, everyone has different pain points and a unique set of needs.

Helping your company's stakeholders adjust to a new reality requires strong leadership. This includes small "L" leadership (individual contributors demonstrating the right attitude and mindset) as well as big "L" leadership from those in the C-suite and senior management. Of course, in order for leaders to drive change, they need to be bought in themselves.

Here's a rundown of the key players you need to win over to ensure your Intelligent Revenue program sees the light of day.

- **The Chief Sales Officer (CSO).** This leader will be most interested in the planning and forecasting improvements that Intelligent Revenue offers. This can be a tricky leader to pin down, largely due to the unpredictable nature of the role. Some CSOs perform in vastly different ways at different companies. What accounts for the discrepancy? Do they behave differently depending on the company, or is it the environment? Is it the data and tools? Is it the culture? Get to the heart of what makes your CSO tick and convince them that IR will offer them an opportunity to be more effective in their role and improve sales culture.
- **The VP of Sales.** Like the CSO, the VP of sales will fixate on planning and forecasting your revenue operation with increased certainty. The VP of sales, however, is likely going to need more convincing, since they will be naturally suspicious that any new tech tool could actually bring value—or worse, that these tools could replace them. Fortunately, once you understand their fears, the conversation is rela-

tively simple: Intelligent Revenue promises augmentation, not replacement. It's an additional data point to use in conjunction with their expertise, not a way for a computer to eliminate their job.

- **Sales Managers.** It can be difficult to persuade this group of leaders that there is an infinitely better way than the manual method they're deeply involved and invested in. They tend to get in the weeds when confronted with a new tool, spouting out endless what-ifs to prove that automation can't actually do everything they do manually—which, of course, it can.

- **The Chief Financial Officer (CFO) and VP of Finance.** These leaders will gravitate toward the planning and forecasting possibilities. Skeptics at heart, they're also not usually too excited about making a switch. It's easy to understand why. CFOs don't want to be sold a bill of goods, especially when they've already invested a tremendous amount in a CRM that was supposed to improve sales. They need help connecting the dots to see how an Intelligent Revenue approach can leverage their CRM much more effectively and drive productivity improvements.

- **The Chief Information Officer (CIO).** Some people joke that CIO really stands for "career is over." CIOs usually come in to take on big reengineering projects to fix a company's broken systems. Usually, they get about a year to a year-and-a-half to realize their vision. With such a narrow window and a lot riding on their success, they're going to be skeptical of anything that could derail their own initiatives. You must convince them that the risk of incorporating a new tool is far outweighed by the potential benefits.

No matter which member of leadership you're trying to convince, remember, it's rarely about the technological piece.

More often, it's the perceived threat a new system poses to their careers. Of course, we've found that Intelligent Revenue isn't a career killer at all, but rather a career accelerator. When you're able to drive the behaviors you want, close more valuable deals, and, most importantly, make your number, then the trust and respect you'll gain in your organization and in your industry will only grow.

And if they're still not convinced? Remind them—sales leaders in particular—that they can hoard their magic formula all they want. The whole organization doesn't have to know how the VP of sales keeps calling the ball with such efficiency. It could simply be their secret weapon for making great decisions. For all anyone else knows, a shift to Intelligent Revenue hasn't changed anything—they've just gotten extra brilliant.

#3: WHAT'S THE CURRENT STATE OF YOUR REVENUE OPERATION?

When working with new clients, we often encounter one of two fundamental challenges with their revenue operation—or sometimes their entire business model.

First, there's the data. No organization's data is in great shape when they first begin to adopt an Intelligent Revenue program. For most organizations, this data has been housed in spreadsheets. It's incomplete. It's full of errors. It's easy to break with the slightest spreadsheet manipulation.

The less attention you've paid to your data, the more you can expect some extensive massaging or cleaning just to prepare it for the IR process. Take care of the necessary hygiene, and you can feel confident that the automation works efficiently. From there, you can shift your focus to analyzing the output and figuring out whether people are doing what they're supposed to.

Second, there's the issue with strategy. As I mentioned earlier, you can absolutely automate a bad plan. It's not the best idea, but it's still an improvement over a spreadsheet. When we see organizations trying to automate bad plans, most often the issue is that the compensation plan is overcomplicated (see Chapter 5).

We'll talk more in the next chapter about how to get the most out of your automation. More crucial than the *what*, however, is the *why*. What is your strategy, why did you choose it, and are there opportunities to better focus your approach?

#4: WHAT'S YOUR EMPLOYEE EXPERIENCE?

It's easy to think that the talent crisis began with the COVID-19 pandemic and the subsequent Great Resignation from 2020 to 2022. In truth, CEOs have been struggling to attract and retain the right talent for just about all of the twenty-first century, if not longer.

This issue isn't likely to go away anytime soon—that is, if you don't flip the script on your employee experience. Rather than focusing on stopping people from leaving, how can you create the experience and environment that makes people (especially your sales reps) want to stay because they enjoy the work? How can you help them to not only spread their wings, but to have confidence in the leadership team, organizational strategy, and so on?

As we discussed in previous chapters, Intelligent Revenue's improved structure will go a long way in this effort. When the members of your revenue operation have greater transparency into your strategy, your decision-making processes, and the systems driving it, they'll feel much more confident about their job as a whole. However, you can do more—fix your comp plan, ditch the hero culture, and stop attrition—all of which we'll discuss in the next few chapters.

TAKE THE CHANCE

As you look at the state of your own organization, specific needs within your revenue operation, and the likely receptiveness of both leadership and the broader culture, you may be wondering whether an Intelligent Revenue approach is the right move for you.

I can't answer that for you. I'm biased. I think IR is for everyone. If you're on the fence about what to do, however, ask yourself two questions:

- Do I see the opportunity that IR presents?
- Am I willing to take the risk on something new?

To the second question, I want to be clear that the risk isn't with Intelligent Revenue itself, but with the receptivity of the culture adopting it. We know what this approach can do, and we've seen the difference it can make for all kinds of organizations.

However, we understand that, to most people, this is new territory. And in order to be successful with any new system, you must have both the vision and the desire to make it work. From there, you'll want to first get your essential stakeholders on board with Intelligent Revenue and begin the process of translating and operationalizing your processes to get people working and behaving in the desired way.

That can be a hard lift. Moreover, it can take time. While not a two-year transformation, adopting Intelligent Revenue isn't a two-month effort either. Expect the transition to take a while.

CASE STUDY: CI INVESTMENTS

Founded in 1965, CI Investments is a finance company focusing on global asset management. In 2021, as part of a planned expansion, the company began focusing on accelerating operations across divisions and enhancing workflows.

In a post-pandemic landscape, that hasn't always been the easiest task. Committed to building the agility necessary to manage their revenue intelligently, CI Investments partnered with Xactly to adopt the necessary tools and infrastructure.

With the right systems in place, CI Investments then turned their attention to using their data more strategically to align their production and revenue streams. They achieved this in three ways:

- Assess results daily in order to remain agile and make impactful changes to sales plans when necessary
- Deliver increased clarity to both sales team members and executive stakeholders
- Reverse engineer workflows from forecasts to achieve key objectives

The change was dramatic. Through improved revenue predictability and forecasting abilities, the CI Investments team was now able to look at trend lines and historical data and easily forecast revenue with accuracy.

The benefits don't stop there. Since implementing an Intelligent Revenue system and framework, CI Investments has seen:

- A 10 percent reduction in errors, saving the company tens of thousands of dollars in the process
- A 20 percent improvement in forecasting accuracy, which has led to a comprehensive understanding of compensation structures
- Increased trust, transparency, and collaboration between the finance and sales departments
- An enhanced reputation and brand to attract and retain top performers

Finally, CI Investments can also accurately assess the effectiveness of performance-related variable compensation, enabling them to make sales decisions with significantly higher precision and reliable outputs for the company. The result? A business and a revenue operation that are resilient enough to withstand internal and external change.

To get there, we recommend an agile approach. Develop the sprint teams necessary to take the project from start to finish, and then start executing. Uncertainty is a constant in the business world, but it shouldn't paralyze you. Attempt to integrate the best solutions to your problems, get data-driven feedback, and adjust accordingly.

Now that you understand the value of Intelligent Revenue and where your own organization stands, let's start upgrading your revenue operation for the twenty-first century. In the first chapter of Part 2, I will show you how to transform your organization from a team of spreadsheet monkeys to Intelligent Revenue thought leaders.

INTELLIGENT REVENUE TUNE-UPS

→ Where does your company stack up on the Maturity Model?

→ What factors within your organization are holding you back from where you want to go? How can you overcome them?

→ What one step can you take today to move closer to your company's endgame?

PART 2

OPTIMIZING
FOR GROWTH
AND
SUSTAINABILITY

CHAPTER 4

GET OUT OF THE STONE AGE

IT'S THE 2020S. WHY ARE YOU STILL MANAGING YOUR revenue operation on spreadsheets?

Is it because you like spreadsheets?

Can't be. Everyone I know who's ever used a spreadsheet has had more than a few colorful words for them when a cell didn't populate or an important calculation misfired.

Is it because they're convenient?

Again, can't be. An effective spreadsheet takes a ton of time to set up—and even more time to make sure it's performing. Besides, there's no automation; anytime you need to refresh a spreadsheet with new information, you have to manually input the information (and pray you don't break the spreadsheet in the process).

Is it because they're the devil you know?

I'm willing to bet that's it. After all, if you aren't aware of what other solutions are out there, what choice do you have but to grin and bear it?

Spreadsheets were game changers when they were introduced. They've been ubiquitous in the business world for so long that many of us take their very presence for granted. Plus, they're familiar—and we humans are naturally resistant to change.

Many areas of business have moved on from spreadsheets and into the cloud-based, AI-powered, and data-driven SaaS world that we explored in the last chapter. But for most companies, their revenue operation is still stuck on spreadsheets—in other words, still trapped in the Stone Age.

Think about your own revenue operation. How many crucial functions depend on spreadsheets for you to execute them? I'm willing to bet that every single one is at least somewhat spreadsheet dependent.

Now, think about the financial implications of this. If you're a large organization, then you're calculating millions—if not billions—of dollars worth of data using technology that's essentially held together with twigs and bubble gum. That's a lot of money to leave to the whims of such a flawed and clunky system.

The question is: Why is this happening? With the whole business world now seemingly driven by the many different SaaS solutions out there, how is it that so many businesses have allowed such a crucial area of their business to remain so vulnerable to error?

Again, blame it on the devil you know.

In my first book, I referred to this as "paving the cow paths." When cows are kept in a pasture for a period of time, they settle on a certain way to get from point A to point B. After they walk this route long enough, they wear a path into the dirt. It may not be the best route, but it's the one they've become used to following. If a farmer were then to come by and pave those paths, sure, they may be helping in one regard. But did they ever stop to consider whether that path was the right one to follow?

Unfortunately, we pave the cow paths in business all too often. We tend to follow the same routes over and over, hoping to get better performance every time while doing nothing to actually change our approach and facilitate that change.

Sound familiar? That's also one description people use to define insanity.

It's not enough to attempt to do the best version of what you've always done. You're not going to accomplish anything new until you begin to think differently about what you've been doing. As we'll see in this chapter, when you ignore the solution that's right in front of you, the consequences don't just impact you and your teams, but also any other team who depends on your results.

Sadly, this happens all the time in most revenue operations. It's likely happening to you—and costing you a lot of money. After you've seen all the ways you're paying for your addiction to spreadsheets and silos, you'll understand just how bad the problem is.

A noticeable shift away from the old way of doing things is already upon us.

According to a 2022 Gartner survey, 46 percent of CEOs plan to scale up their enterprise's digital initiatives. Further, in the next two years, 85 percent of CFOs plan to boost their investments in digital capabilities, with nearly a quarter of those CFOs citing increased automation as a key area of focus.

The good news, then, is that clearly the C-suite is ready to throw money at this problem. They understand that building a quality business today looks different than it used to, and they want to get out ahead of the change.

The bad news is that (1) there are a lot of problems that need to be fixed, and (2) not all executives realize the importance of automating key aspects of their revenue operation.

This begs the question: While the C-suite may be committed to spending serious money on digital initiatives in the near future, what are they going to spend that money on? Who in the organization will benefit most?

Answering the first question usually leads to an answer for the second question. Those answers tend to be consistent across the companies we work with.

For most organizations, the first step to adopting an Intelligent Revenue approach is simple: stop relying on antiquated systems and start embracing modern tools and automation. This alone will improve your year-over-year revenue growth before you get out of bed in the morning.

GET YOUR APPS IN GEAR

There are a gazillion SaaS apps out there. According to Salesforce, the average sales team uses at least ten sales tools to close a deal—from CRM to marketing automation.[14]

I think that survey is undercounting. At Xactly, we have twenty-five different SaaS apps tied to our sales operation alone.

So how did we get here?

With the proliferation of accessible internet in the past two decades, telecommunications companies took the obvious next step—virtualization. Physical hardware was prohibitively expensive at this point, and it made sense to offer software to end users via the internet. Several companies saw this as a way to save money and improve offerings and, thus, modern cloud computing was born.[15]

---

14 Adam Gilberd, "10 Statistics That Reveal the Future of Sales," Salesforce, February 28, 2023, https://www.salesforce.com/blog/15-sales-statistics/.

15 IBM, "Cloud Computing: A Complete Guide," accessed September 8, 2023, https://www.ibm.com/cloud/learn/cloud-computing-gbl.

With the move to the cloud, companies now had access to the tools and raw processing power not only to meet their prior needs, but to pursue solutions that they never thought possible. Driving this pursuit was a singular promise: automation. How could businesses execute everyday tasks and complex processes both more efficiently and more effectively?

This one simple question gave rise to a new industry—software as a service (or *SaaS* as it is more commonly known)—and in the early days, everyone and their dog wanted in on the action. Anyone with a half-decent idea was making an app—and since "half-decent" is subjective, there were some pretty ridiculous ideas. Phoenix, Delite, and MyCity were all fun ideas, but none were strategic or useful. Other products, like Tali, Transpose, and Ansaro, had promise but ultimately failed. Automation for automation's sake, it turned out, wasn't much of a value-add at all.

By the time companies started wising up to this, several years had passed—and the problem had multiplied. For most companies, it wasn't just one redundant app in the chain; it was several. Of the fifty or so applications a company might have in their tool chain, only about ten were doing any real work!

Still, that wasn't the worst of it. Yes, there were too many damn apps, but the real problem was that none of them were talking to each other. Sure, it was great that a company's CRM had a whole host of data on its buyers, but none of the other forty-nine apps could access it.

What good are fifty different apps working without anything resembling cohesion or synchronization? Today's business world is marked by way too much data and not enough time to process it all. This calls for serious help, and having fifty different silos of data that get processed in fifty different unique ways isn't helpful.

Think of what makes a silo useful—it's sealed off from everything around it. You need tools that perform different tasks, but wouldn't you much rather they work with one another? How would you like to sift through reports from fifty different unintegrated apps every morning?

I'm on a mission to drastically cut that number—not because they're bad, but because it's too much. You could have fifty vendors providing fifty different apps. And while each of those apps may be useful in some narrow function, most are focused on delivering data when what most businesses really want is *information*.

Now, I'm not suggesting that you go from fifty vendors to one overnight. There are some fantastic providers out there, but I don't believe any of those providers will do a perfect job of solving every business need that you have.

Instead, I'm suggesting that you look for vendors that provide multiple de-siloed solutions.

Intelligent Revenue relies on using tools that allow your operation to work smarter, not using tools for tools' sake. A de-siloed strategy allows you to focus on the tools that can integrate with one another and to slowly phase out those that don't. This approach will make your operation not only more efficient, but overall better.

To many business leaders, automation is exciting. But don't get carried away. A de-siloed solution is always about automating for the business's sake. Embracing the SaaS-based ecosystem does wonders for many companies, but the best adopters want to get even more value out of these systems so they aren't just more effective, but smarter.

AUTOMATE LIKE YOU MEAN IT

Remember the days of paper maps? Some of you might not, but I'm guessing most of you still do. Paper maps did serve their purpose; if you knew how to read them, then you could get where you were trying to go, but it took much more effort. First, you had to find your map from wherever you last tucked it away. Then you had to find the address of whatever destination you were going to. Then you needed to carefully trace out a route from point A to point B, writing down a step-by-step path as you went.

Again, the process worked, but there were several opportunities to introduce problems or errors. What if one of the streets on your route turned out to be one-way? What if a road was closed due to construction? What if your route took you through the highest-traffic part of town during rush hour?

It's no wonder that people were so excited when tools like MapQuest came along. Sure, you still had to look up the address ahead of time. And sure, driving while trying to follow a hand-held printout wasn't the easiest. But at least the directions were all automated—and a little less error-prone than if you had looked at a map.

MapQuest was a lot like the paved cow paths we discussed at the beginning of the chapter—better than nothing, but not a great solution. A cow path isn't necessarily smart or efficient. Often, it's neither. Likewise, MapQuest was more effective than driving blindly, but making a paper map digital failed to solve the actual problems—ease of use and accounting for real-time factors.

MapQuest automated a system that wasn't smart or efficient, but it didn't change the game. It paved over a dirt path and called it a day. Luckily, that wasn't the end of this story.

Flash forward to today, and AI-driven navigation apps make

getting from point A to B easier than ever. Directions are immediate, apps guide your navigation in real time, and you even get instant alerts for traffic, accidents, speed traps, and so on. After using such a powerful, intuitive tool, how could you ever go back to the world of paper maps?

This same evolution can be seen in how sales leaders administer their comp plans. Here, many organizations are still in the world of paper maps, or at best, MapQuest. They may have automated, but not in a way that changes the game. Manually assigning a sales plan to each member of your sales team takes time—especially if you manage a sales team of two hundred people or more. It's neither particularly fun nor a good use of anyone's bandwidth.

An Intelligent Revenue approach emphasizes automating that entire process. As soon as you're ready to hit "go" on the new comp plan, your de-siloed tools will pull the relevant names from your system and assign the new comp plan to every team member in one quick move. Less time, better accuracy, and greater peace of mind. Even better, dynamic tools update automatically. Whenever you experience turnover, for instance, the system removes that rep from the plan, maintaining up-to-date records of who's assigned to what, as well as where they are in their own comp plan.

Of course, automation alone doesn't mean you're suddenly a champion of Intelligent Revenue. You could still be the farmer paving the cow paths. If you're still working off an unsophisticated go-to-market strategy or compensation plan, then you're merely automating a flawed system. That's better than nothing—and it will go a long way in reducing error rates, dangling the carrot for your sales team, and increasing transparency across the board. But as we'll explore in greater detail in Chapter 5, Intelligent Revenue can do much more than that.

Where our system separates itself, and why good automation often leads to exponentially improved results, is converting shared data into usable information.

TAKE CHARGE OF YOUR DATA

How do you determine equitable territories for everyone on your sales team? Data.

How do you calculate accurate compensation payouts and drive the behaviors that align with your CEO's top priorities? Again, data.

How do you help your sales leaders solve their forecasting problems? Data.

Of course, raw data isn't going to solve the problem either. Not too long ago, data lakes were all the rage. In fact, for many organizations, they still are. Over time, however, many organizations have found that when you throw everything into one big dataset, you end up with less of a lake and more of a swamp. Ask anybody who's tried: it's not easy to slog through the muck to find the right bits of data and figure out how they connect.

These aren't the kinds of problems you can simply throw bodies at. More people using more sophisticated spreadsheets won't help. You need better data, better processes, better training, and better leadership.

So, to recap: combating your revenue problems with manpower won't get you far. Collecting large amounts of unsorted data won't help either—and using employees to sort all the data will barely make a dent. But combine that data with tools that can drive new insights, and suddenly you have a considerable competitive advantage.

All of that collected data is derived primarily from the way we do business. The move to the cloud may have been driven by a desire to decentralize systems and automate processes, but as it turned out, there was an even greater benefit: data.

For a long time, business has been more or less a guessing game; you stick your thumb in the air, try to see which way the wind is blowing, and let your gut drive decisions based on what little predictive information you have available. In the early years, Xactly followed this procedure just like every other SaaS provider out there. We didn't treat the mountains of data we were accumulating through our product as inherently useful, predictive information—it was an afterthought. Cloud-based apps were the first technology to collect anonymous user data on this scale, but it took a company with the foresight to prioritize this data for it to matter.

This isn't to discount the value of going with your gut, of course. Intuition has long been understood as a valuable decision-making tool. However, gut instincts work best when a company is in its infancy. As a company grows, relying on the people with good intuition isn't scalable. There are simply too many people involved in day-to-day decision-making for this to work.

What if a company had the ability to aggregate information and drive new insights in a way that had never been possible before? We could use the insights from data to supercharge our process, turning intuition into intelligent decisions with less course correction along the way. Business will never be a no-risk game, but leveraging this strategy would allow us to win a lot more often.

This was our "eureka" moment. One day—quite literally—my business partner and I looked at each other and said, "Holy shit, we're producing and collecting all this data—and it could be very, *very* useful for us."

I imagine many across Silicon Valley and the rest of the

world had similar moments because, right around that time, everything began moving quickly once again. Suddenly, data was all the rage, and the SaaS market split into the haves and the have-nots. The "have-not" group had some impressive tools, but they lacked the data—or the rights to that data—to drive results. The "have" group had ridiculous amounts of data—and all the rights in the world.

The "have-nots" didn't go away. They did whatever they could to obfuscate the fact that they lacked an empirical dataset. This tactic confused the market, blurring the lines between haves and have-nots.

Once the SaaS industry realized the importance of all this data, the game became all about analytics. Who could offer the best insights in the most digestible and actionable context possible?

Many companies failed, and still fail, to grasp the difference between analyzing their own data and being able to compare their data against a benchmark of other, similar companies. These companies don't know how to how to separate insights from measuring performance. That matters because these are two very different things. All the internal insights in the world may not tell you that you stack up poorly with competitors. Market performance data may not be useful in the context of getting your company where it's trying to go.

Knowing the difference between the two is critical.

Enter artificial intelligence (AI) and machine learning. AI is humankind's best attempt so far at replicating the adaptability of intelligent beings, and machine learning is an offshoot of that science, focusing on recognizing patterns and making meaning out of all that information.

A well-designed AI tool can scrutinize data on a massive scale—far beyond what we humans are capable of achieving—

and generate insights that we would have been otherwise blind to. Even better, these tools are always learning and evolving. The more data you feed them and the longer you allow them to run, the better they get.

You probably already know this part of the story, since AI and machine learning get an outsized share of press. But as important as AI models are, they aren't the "voilà" moment of the magic trick; they're merely the software behind it. As we and other developers learned fairly quickly, machine learning tools are relatively easy to build, almost trivial.

Owning a dataset robust enough upon which to apply the AI and machine learning models against is the secret. Data is the secret that turns AI and machine learning into a competitive advantage. As the prominent data scientist Matthew Emerick said, "Data is the nutrition of artificial intelligence. When an AI eats junk food, it's not going to perform very well."[16] Fortunately, we had the data.

Once these systems began to show revolutionary results, there was a stampede. A new gold rush. Today, in terms of pure value proposition, data is the fuel that powers new economic value creation. Think of data like the new oil, untapped before the Industrial Revolution and then suddenly indispensable. And yet, despite the tremendous benefits we have seen as a result of this data explosion, we still have not unlocked data's full potential in a way that benefits all areas of an organization. In fact, in the case of driving an organization's revenue operations, we've barely even tried.

We'll talk more about that throughout the book. For now, let's refocus on the other big problem of the SaaS explosion of the past two decades: siloing.

---

16 Coresignal, "20 Data Science Quotes by Industry Experts," *Coresignal* (blog), January 24, 2023, https://coresignal.com/blog/data-science-quotes/.

CASE STUDY: HYATT HOTELS

The Chicago-based Hyatt Hotels Corporation is a leading global hospitality company with a portfolio of twenty premier brands—including more than 875 properties in over sixty countries across six continents as of 2019. Hyatt is a deeply mission-driven company, focused on taking care of people so they can be their best. This purpose informs all the company's business decisions and growth strategy, allowing them to attract and retain top colleagues, build relationships with guests, and create value for shareholders.

When Hyatt first began working with Xactly, they were deeply focused on their "need for the now." In the hospitality business, their sellers were focused on getting instant results—whether in terms of accrual or just making sure their production was accurate. Unfortunately, because their sales team was still largely operating off of spreadsheets, the Hyatt team found those instant results all but impossible to achieve. And with a sales team of over 1,200 people, compensation accuracy had also become a big problem.

After partnering with Xactly, Hyatt was able to implement a new SMP system that helped them not only stay on time with payments but also drive the right behaviors among their sales team. This allowed Hyatt to reduce their time to close the quarter from six to eight weeks down to only a few weeks.

Further, the system made it far easier for the company to pay their reps on time—and accurately—by the end of every month. This has gone a long way in establishing trust by creating a system and a process that allows sellers to know exactly where they stand at all times.

DE-SILO YOUR SYSTEMS

When everyone has a SaaS product, and everyone wants to add that product to your software stack, you're bound to encounter not only some bloat, but a little bit of an operational headache. Siloed apps that can't talk to each other are one thing—siloed apps that can't share data across platforms are another.

To be fair, even siloed data is still useful. It's certainly better than no data. However, it's no match for broad-based organizational data that is shared across the many different functions of a business. Sales data informs forecasting tools. Forecasting tools inform go-to-market tools. Go-to-market tools inform sales comp tools. And so on. That's the ideal, but for most organizations, that's not the reality.

It's no surprise, then, that today's businesses want fewer vendors—only one neck to choke, as it were—and data that is clean and utilized across the entire platform. The days of the single-point SaaS product are over—or at least, they soon will be.

Here's why. Imagine that your chief revenue officer is looking for a new SaaS product to help with forecasting. In your search, you find two solutions. Both are AI-powered and data-driven. Both deliver valuable insights. Both would help your CRO call the ball more accurately.

For one vendor, that's all their product does—and it costs twice as much. For the other vendor, forecasting is just one feature in a suite of tools that also includes sales planning and compensation—and because these tools are all connected, they all draw from the same robust dataset.

This doesn't mean I'm advocating for a single vendor that fulfills every Intelligent Revenue need. For most of the companies we work with, that isn't realistic. Rather, this is a wake-up call that trimming the fat could be very beneficial—say, from forty-five vendors to twenty. Less can be more if the tools and data are optimized.

Suddenly, it's not just about calling the ball, but about knowing exactly how you're going to get there. For instance, if your reps are calling the ball on sixty deals, the platform might calculate that fifty-eight of those deals will actually go through, based on pattern recognition and other elements. That's great—but because the platform is also tied into both the sales planning and sales comp data, it can determine the following:

- Exactly which sales reps will close those fifty-eight deals
- The exact commission plans each of those reps is on and where they are in their year against those plans
- The company's exact commission expense exposure once those fifty-eight deals close

Then, of course, all that data feeds into the planning cycle for the next go-round. Your CSO, for one, is going to be much more informed and prepared. They'll know how to deploy the sales force more efficiently and effectively, because it won't be guesswork anymore. Even better, this data can also help you generate a commission expense forecast for your CFO that (1) most don't presently have, and (2) is impossible to generate with a siloed forecasting system.

Again, just like with the spreadsheet scenario we used to open the chapter, the choice is obvious; the interconnected platform wins every time.

This is where the market is heading. And while it's difficult to say exactly where it will all lead, it seems like a no-brainer to foresee that this future will hold far fewer "one-trick pony" companies. Why work with thirty different vendors that each offer a siloed solution when you can work with one or two vendors in a more integrated and intelligent way?

When you can integrate the same data across the different functions of your revenue operation, then your data becomes much more informative. A siloed piece of data is interesting in and of itself. It can be useful. But when that piece of data is part of an integrated platform, then it becomes something you can actively use to drive revenue. If that isn't a value-add, then I don't know what is.

However, companies have had to deal with siloed solutions for so long that they've become part of the landscape—and in the case of your revenue operation, those silos are still part of the problem.

Ripping off the Band-Aid and de-siloing isn't easy, especially when nonintegrated tools still seem effective. It takes realizing that merely being effective isn't good enough when competitors are taking advantage of a *more effective* way.

DE-SILOED FUNCTIONS ACROSS THE REVENUE OPERATION

Before coming to work with Xactly, one of our clients used a stand-alone application for quota and territory planning. It was an effective tool, but also highly complex to manage. Worse, it was siloed. Sharing information from this tool to other tools in the chain required a lot of clunky, manual effort.

As it happened, they were already on the path to Intelligent Revenue when it came to incentive compensation and automating commissions. Once they saw how one tool could integrate not only with other tools in their chain, but also with other functions such as commissions and forecasting, they fully committed to IR.

Now able to integrate across functions, the company could run quotas and territories with ease. They could enable self-service in the field for sales managers to input their data to a centralized hub. At every touch point, managers could receive updates and check the quotas.

In a de-siloed revenue operation, the exchange of information is reciprocal. Instead of emails flying back and forth, all the data use occurs within a self-contained, integrated application. The sales input, in turn, feeds into the compensation module. One standardized platform does all this work.

The secret sauce lies in gathering all the data from different inputs—quotas, territories, and commissions, to name a few. Then over time, as more data is aggregated, an Intelligent Revenue approach will be able to take a historical view as well as offer future projections. Even more importantly, you can compare performance to peers, giving you the advantage of benchmarking how you're doing with your systems of record. And all of this information becomes visible across your organization.

GREATER TRANSPARENCY

Your revenue operation should mirror the Intelligent Revenue approach as a whole—sharing valuable information across departments and levels in a way that promotes company, and individual, success. Imagine a world where your sales reps can see exactly what they will make—and how to make more—on any given sale and in real time.

The alignment of company and individual goals is a top priority of Intelligent Revenue, and it's not only possible but easy with a de-siloed operation.

Think from a sales rep's perspective. They can complete all their day-to-day functions in one virtual place and receive the information they need in multiple formats. Forecasting then links to both the CRM and pattern recognition to tell reps what they should try to sell and how to change their approach to close the deal.

To make effective recommendations, this AI-driven pattern-recognition tool analyzes over sixty different inputs to create a holistic, 360 degree view of the sale. It examines inputs like sentiment analysis of email traffic between the rep and prospect, sentiment analysis of the recorded sales calls (Chorus), adherence to sales methodologies, momentum gauged by prospect engagement and interaction, ideal customer profile (ICP), as well as unique prospect data like win rates against a particular customer. Then it matches those inputs against known patterns and best practices and notifies the rep on how their behavior may need to change.

Once they close the deal, reps can access all details via a centralized dashboard, including a detailed breakdown of their check. Reps are able to compare their performance to others, and managers can assess overall team or rep performance at any time. Best of all, managers can use this information as a coaching tool to fine-tune the revenue engine.

How does this lead to Intelligent Revenue? Again, it comes back to dangling that carrot—aligning your revenue operation with your company's endgame. When sales leadership and the sales team alike have greater visibility, greater accountability, and higher trust, when they can see in real-time the exact moves they can make to benefit the company and improve their own commission, they put in better effort in less time to generate higher-quality revenue.

NOT YOUR PROBLEM? ACTUALLY, IT IS

If you've never seen the pinch points to your revenue operation laid out like this, you're not alone. Even in a relatively connected and interdependent organization, challenges like this often get siloed. For more of us, it's far too easy to ignore the big picture and focus only on the piece of the pie that we're responsible for.

It doesn't have to be so hard. All it requires is some level of alignment and commitment among leadership between the CFO, the CRO, and the CSO. To get that alignment, first it's important to realize how interconnected the different areas of your kingdom actually are. What affects one affects the other. For instance, the CSO may own the forecast, but the CFO depends on that forecast to make important financial decisions for the business. No one is asking the CFO to call the ball, of course, but what if everyone was working from the same tool set and had greater visibility into how decisions were being made in each sector of the revenue operation?

I'm not describing a fantasy world here. As you'll see in the next chapter, the opportunity for this kind of alignment already exists. All you have to do is look up, recognize that opportunity, and act on it.

There's a famous comic where two cavemen are pushing a cart with square wheels. Beside them stands a third caveman holding two round wheels. But the other two cavemen won't pay any attention to him.

"No thanks!" says one.

"We are too busy!" says the other.

And off they go, stumbling forward into the world on their cart with square wheels.

Do those two cavemen love the slow progress they're making?

Of course not. But they're too caught up in their work and the clunky system they've adopted to realize that a better solution is already right there waiting for them.

So why are you still using spreadsheets? Why hasn't your revenue operation embraced the twenty-first century like the rest of your organization? Most likely, it's because you're too caught up in your work to realize that there's a better way.

But if you've read this far, then by now you understand that the old way isn't getting you as far as it could. It's impossible to halt progress, and refusing to get ahead will only leave you further behind. In the next chapter, we'll begin to explore exactly what the shiny new wheels of Intelligent Revenue can get you.

INTELLIGENT REVENUE TUNE-UPS

→ What tools are most important to your business, and what functions would most help drive revenue?

→ What solutions could help to accomplish those goals?

→ Do these solutions run on the same platform—or at the very least, can they talk to each other?

→ How will transparency and de-siloing overhaul your revenue operation?

CHAPTER 5

FIX YOUR COMP PLAN

CLIFF YOUNG WAS A SIXTY-ONE-YEAR-OLD FARMER LIVING in the outback of Australia.

He did not have fancy shoes or professional training. He was just a guy who ran around his farm all day and had taken an interest in marathon running at an age when most people start slowing down.

So when the opportunity came to enter the Sydney to Melbourne Ultramarathon in 1983, he thought, *Why the hell not?*

As he told the dubious press ahead of the race,

> I grew up on a farm where we couldn't afford horses or tractors, and the whole time I was growing up, whenever the storms would roll in, I'd have to go out and round up the sheep. We had two thousand sheep on two thousand acres. Sometimes I would have to run those sheep for two or three days. It took

a long time, but I'd always catch them. I believe I can run this race.[17]

Cliff's belief in himself was well placed. He didn't just complete the race. He didn't just *win* the race. He set the world record for what some have called the most grueling ultramarathon in the world—beating the previous record by nearly *two days*.

How did he do it?

Simple: he didn't sleep.

Up to that point, ultramarathoners all operated on the assumption that they should get six hours of sleep a night. Without a coach and with very little in terms of formal training, Cliff had no such assumption. Sure, he ran slower than everyone else, but he also ran for days without interruption. And that combination helped him shatter all previous records.

Of course, his record didn't stand for long. Once professional athletes learned that they didn't actually need to sleep six hours a night, they quickly adopted his approach and beat his time. But the fact that they went so long without doing something that they were actually capable of reveals something important about the human mind.

When someone tells us something that sounds like the truth, we believe it. Sometimes this can be beneficial—we should all believe the person who tells us that jumping off a cliff will kill us, for instance. But sometimes, that supposed truth is limiting. If you believe the body requires sleep and that you cannot run twenty-four hours a day, then you'll focus on how tired you are and how much you need rest. When that truth gets shattered, the paradigm shifts.

---

17 Elite Feet, "The Legend of Cliff Young: The 61-Year-Old Farmer Who Won the World's Toughest Race," accessed September 1, 2022, https://elitefeet.com/the-legend-of-cliff-young/.

Now, let's put this in sales terms.

Say that I have a team of sales reps who are all used to hitting their quotas by selling low-margin deals that renew annually. If I tell them that the best way to hit their numbers and make the most money is by selling five-year contracts with a 5 percent annual increase, they're liable to mutiny. No salesperson in their right mind would agree to such a crazy idea.

Actually, the Rule of X isn't a crazy idea. Assuming it can't work is just another self-limiting belief—and we have the benchmark data to prove it. Not only can a sales team operate while prioritizing five-year contracts with annual 5 percent increases, they can thrive. The only reason no one was doing it before was that they didn't believe it was possible.

This gets us to the core question of this chapter: How do you incentivize your sales reps to change their behaviors so that their performance aligns with your Intelligent Revenue goals—no matter how crazy they might seem to your reps?

Certainly this isn't an easy task. Sales reps, as a group, are suspicious of change. They're conditioned to believe that any time they try new things, they put their income at risk. Of course, that's a nonstarter. Perhaps more than any other profession, a seller's income relies on their own ability to do the hard work—more specifically, to grind out those sales any way they can and at the highest possible payout for themselves.

Traditionally, this has been known as "gaming the plan." If you were to ask most CFOs, this mindset is the bane of their existence, destroying the organization's ability to earn high-quality revenue. However, in my first book, *Game the Plan*, I argue that it doesn't have to be so. If you're incentivizing your sales reps to drive the behaviors that get you the results you want, then gaming the plan can actually be a *good* thing.

This progressive vision of a type of sales comp that is focused on aligning behavior is Xactly's heritage. Rather than treating your sales reps as coin operated, this approach empowers your sales reps to drive the results you want.

To do that, however, they need to understand your business's goals and how their own behaviors impact those goals. What does your organization want? Are you going after new names? Are you mining your existing installed base for more business? Do you want to introduce a new product and make a market for it? Are you trying to deposition a competitor?

In this chapter, we'll explore how the Intelligent Revenue framework builds off the game-the-plan mentality I advocate for in my first book by driving performance. In an Intelligent Revenue comp system, the leadership team decides the priorities and designs a system of incentives to drive target behaviors from their sales reps. Then an Intelligent Revenue system provides added transparency so the rep can not only receive helpful prompts to help them align with organizational goals and close more deals, but can also track their progress toward their own goals in real time.

Like we discussed in Chapter 2, those organizational goals should follow the Rule of X. We prioritize multiyear contracts with fixed, annual increases, because we know that not all deals are created equal. This kind of thinking not only helps your organization, but it helps your clients.

As we move through the following strategies, remember: automating alone will fix many of the problems inherent in your comp plan—but not all of them. There's still the human part of the equation. To change your results, then, don't focus on tools. Focus on behaviors.

REESTABLISH TRUST BETWEEN SALES AND FINANCE

We're only human, and mistakes are bound to happen in an operation without automated safeguards. It's all too easy to type the wrong number into a spreadsheet or mess up a calculation. The problem is, even small mistakes add up and become detrimental to a company's bottom line. They also ebb away at trust—between leadership and reps, and between the sales and finance departments. Our goal is alignment throughout an organization, and reps are happier, not to mention more productive, when they know what's going on regarding compensation. Less errors and more trust go a long way toward a healthier company.

THE 10 PERCENT ERROR RATE

One of the largest expense items at any company is their sales force. Say you have a sales team of about two hundred people. If each of them is making $50,000 to $100,000 in variable pay, then that's a $10 million to $20 million cost center—a pretty significant chunk of change.

You'd assume that with so much money on the line you'd want to manage that cost center as closely and accurately as possible. And yet, study after study shows that the error rate for a typical sales compensation program runs at 10 percent.[18]

If you're hoping that your reps will report these errors, well, you're half-right. Your sales reps *will* report plenty of errors to you...when those errors result in a loss to them. If your reps are running their own books correctly, they'll know exactly when you screwed up in their favor and when you screwed up in your

---

18 Xactly, "When Paying Sales Commissions, 90% Accuracy Is an F," *Xactly* (blog), July 18, 2019, https://www.xactlycorp.com/blog/paying-commissions-90-accuracy-f.

own favor. It's just that, for the most part, they're going to keep their mouths shut with the former and only report the latter.

I'd like to say that I was above such behavior during my time as a salesperson. Sure, I reported the $80,000 bonus I received when it should have been $8,000, but that's only because the error was so egregious that I figured I had no choice. Had the company paid me $9,000 when they should have paid me only $8,000, I would have happily pocketed the difference—or at the very least, I would have assumed that my own calculations were off.

Now, you can take my own experience and multiply that out. Say you have ten other salespeople like me who were paid out $9,000 when they should have received only $8,000. That's an extra $10,000 that you're never going to see again and that you never should have had to pay—and that's just for one payout. If you're running a typical sales organization, the numbers say you're going to make another similar mistake at least once in the next ten payouts. When sales compensation is already such a large expense, do you really want to be paying out tens of thousands of dollars—if not millions—that you don't have to?

SHOW ME (THE EVIDENCE FOR HOW YOU CALCULATED) THE MONEY

When you're running a 10 percent error rate, you're going to be responsible for a lot of commission adjustments each month. But whether you're making fifty adjustments a month or five hundred, both of those numbers are terrible—and a sure sign that your system is all messed up.

If you're using a spreadsheet, two things are likely happening here. First, most of those adjustments—if not all—are the result of human errors that already exist in your spreadsheet. Second, every time you reopen that spreadsheet to make an adjustment, you take the risk of introducing yet another error and yet another bad payout.

Remember, every time you make a commission adjustment, it means that you've paid out someone—or several someones—on your sales team incorrectly. If you're that salesperson, that's an incredibly frustrating situation to be in, a key reason why salespeople like Joan are so willing to listen to other offers when they come around.

Of course, those other firms with their big signing bonuses and bigger payouts are likely working off a similarly broken compensation system. If Joan is going to be frustrated where she works, from her perspective, she's going to make the most possible money doing it.

But just imagine, for a moment, if you didn't have to make commission adjustments five hundred times a month. Imagine if you got it right the first time. If Joan could see that she was being paid fairly, accurately, and on time, then she'd have a lot fewer reasons to leave.

ME AND MY SHADOW ACCOUNTS

Joan would also have a lot more time on her hands. Why? Because she isn't wasting all her time tracking her own commissions on the side—what we often refer to as shadow accounting.

Naturally, no one wants their sales team wasting time running their own spreadsheets. Truth is, salespeople don't either. Any time spent going over the numbers is time spent *not* selling. And last time I checked, I've never met a salesperson who secretly wanted a side job as an accountant. But that's what happens when there's lack of transparency and lack of trust. The second you hear from your buddy that someone in sales comp made an error, you begin doubting your own numbers.

Soon, you've got your own calculations that you're nervously checking against the company's numbers. If you're working in a high-volume company, it's going to take a lot of time to maintain that spreadsheet. And yet, if you're going to catch any errors made by someone in the comp or finance team, you feel like you have no choice.

This isn't a lose-lose scenario just for the sales rep, but also for the people running the books in finance.

I once knew an analyst—we'll call him Gary—who spent a considerable portion of his working hours checking the spreadsheets against the comp plan in order to find any errors. It wasn't that Gary or anyone else in finance were bad at their jobs. It's just that manually entering data into spreadsheets all day is bound to manifest a few errors.

The sales team knew this and didn't trust any of the numbers as a result. This meant they were making constant requests of Gary to double-check the books to make sure they'd been paid out correctly. Suddenly, what was supposed to be a small part of Gary's job took up most of his time.

Most of the time, of course, Gary confirmed that the reps had, in fact, been paid out correctly. But every now and then, Gary would inevitably find an error. The members of the sales team were always grateful for the fix, but each error reinforced the notion that none of the numbers were to be trusted and that everything had to be double-checked.

Our CFO saw all this going on—the time spent double-checking the numbers, the lack of trust, the finger-pointing—and felt helpless. The problem didn't impact only how her team members were spending their time, but also the trust they had in each other to do their jobs correctly. Not only was this game of shadow accounting unsustainable and unscalable, but it was like a poison pill for the organization's culture.

With a centrally managed tool that ran the calculations, auto-populated the data into the correct fields, and then paid the sales team out quickly and accurately, all that mistrust would simply dissolve. If a salesperson is paid $10,000 on a deal and they believe it should have been $11,000, you can point to the specific transaction, the commission rate, the escalators, and anything else used to make the calculation, and verify its accuracy.

In today's data-driven world, it's not enough to shrug and say everything is fine when errors occur. Besides, if you're still working off of spreadsheets, I can assure you that everything is not fine. Manual systems don't allow you to be prescriptive, to create benchmarks, to give your reps real-time access and visibility into how their compensation is calculated. Automated systems can begin to get you there.

Can errors still happen? Sure, even a better system isn't perfect. However, it takes a hell of a lot less time to uncover those errors, and the salesperson at least has a clear basis for reviewing the numbers and determining what went wrong. Instead of simply having a vague feeling that something went wrong, they have full transparency and a path toward resolution.

In order to avoid high turnover among your sales team, this is the environment you must work to create—one where a salesperson can verify their payouts quickly and accurately without resorting to shadow accounting or bugging the analyst a thousand times a day to run the numbers again. With full transparency, all the drama goes away, and the whole culture benefits as a result.

FIX YOUR MEASURES

How many measures should you put on a comp plan in order for it to be effective? Three? Five? Ten? More?

The data is very clear on this. It's three. Anything more, and you're just confusing your sales reps—or at least, obscuring the goal.

Keep it simple. If you're selling tennis shoes, for instance, your measures could be the color of the tennis shoe, the number of shoes you want to sell, and the retail store you want to sell them to. That's it. Nothing more.

We regularly see companies that want to put in twelve measures or more—and they want to automate all of it. While you could make the argument that, hey, at least you're automating, the counterargument is that you're automating a stupid plan. As I like to say at Xactly, you're paving the cow paths. Just because that's the route the cows have always taken doesn't make it the best route. Paving over that route just cements a dubious practice at best.

If you want to automate your dumb plan, be my guest. We can even help you do it. But I'm going to warn you against it. There's very little value in falling in love with some plan that your chief revenue officer (CRO) put together. Yes, CROs have generally been on comp plans their whole lives. But that doesn't mean they know how to design a good comp plan themselves. With all due respect to the many talented CROs out there, most of them don't.

If you're going to break the rules and put more than three measures on a plan, don't make any measure less than 20 percent. Otherwise, that measure simply won't drive the results you're looking for.

DIS-INCENTIVIZE DISCOUNTS

I've talked to thousands of CROs throughout the course of my career. Whenever I ask one of them whether they dis-incentivize their discounts, they always respond emphatically that they do. They're not lying; they believe they do since they're paying on the net discounted amounts.

Unfortunately, they're wrong. Paying on the net deal amount doesn't dis-incentivize your reps from working in their interests instead of the company's interests. The following example shines a light on that.

Imagine you've got a house you'd like to sell. Nothing too fancy, just a nice, established little shack—which, in Silicon Valley, might go for $1 million or more.

You hire a realtor to get that million dollars for you and agree on a 3 percent commission ($30,000) for their troubles. Both you and your realtor know what they're going to get out of the deal. It's a clean, simple understanding.

The next day, your realtor gets an offer on the house for $900,000. What do you think they'll do?

Here's an important psychology lesson. It's easy to assume that the agent would reject that offer, preferring their $30,000 commission over the $27,000 commission they'd get if they sold the house for only $900,000.

But you'd be wrong. Your realtor would be happy to earn $27,000 for a single day's work. They couldn't care less about the extra three grand. They're not going to reject the offer. They're going to come back to you and tell you all the reasons why $900,000 is probably the best you can do.

To the realtor, the convenience of accepting the lower offer (and doing less work) was worth forfeiting the extra income.

So while you lost out on an additional $100,000 (and probably got taken to the cleaners), your realtor is laughing all the way to the bank.

Sounds simple enough when I put it that way, right? Now, here's the problem: this is the exact trap most organizations fall into when they compensate their sales reps by paying on the net.

You may think this is a good way to motivate your reps to stop offering discounts, since the bigger the discount, the smaller the commission. However, just like the realtor, your reps will gladly trade in less work for only marginally smaller payouts. Why? Because discounted deals are easier to close, and a rep can make up for any rate difference by churning out more discounted deals.

That mindset isn't helping your company adopt Intelligent Revenue. Your sales operation will stay stuck where it's always been, and your revenue will remain uncertain.

You can't generate quality revenue if your sales reps are focused on quantity. It just doesn't work. If you want to discourage discounting, then, focus your sales reps on the discounted percentage rather than the discounted amount.

Remember the Rule of X? Ideally, we want the number of years in the contract and the annual rate readjustment to equal ten. But, like we stated earlier, six is neutral. That usually works out as a three-year contract with 3 percent annual rate increases. There's wiggle room with this formula, but only with contract length and annual percentage hikes.

Notice that the deal's total amount doesn't come into play. Any multiyear deal with locked-in annual increases is better than a single-year deal.

There's another factor at play here: reps hate doing math—and they especially hate doing math on the fly in front of a customer. It's much easier for them to calculate and offer a 35 percent discount when a 31 percent discount likely would have closed the deal. Suddenly, your organization is out 4 percent in revenue on the deal for no good reason. Add up these avoidable discounts across the many thousands of deals at a hundred-million-dollar organization, and you can see that's no small drop in the bucket.

Ask yourself, what does your EBITDA look like if you implement a more effective way to dis-incentivize discounts? How many more millions of dollars will end up in your pockets?

And shouldn't your sales reps be able to digest this strategy the moment you've implemented it?

TO CHANGE YOUR COMPANY, CHANGE BEHAVIOR

Some years ago, a well-known bank got in a lot of trouble over how they ran their sales organization. Their goal was well intentioned: they wanted their sales reps to sign new accounts, so they incentivized that behavior.

On its face, this seemed like a good idea. Simple goal, simple incentive, right?

Unfortunately, there was nothing simple about what happened next. While many sales reps proceeded with good intentions, others found a harmful way to game the plan. Since employees were incentivized to open as many accounts as they could, they decided to bypass their customers entirely and simply open new accounts in their names.

Four years and two million fraudulent accounts later, the public finally caught on. By this time, over five thousand bank employees were caught up in the scandal—and promptly terminated once it went public.

The lesson seemed clear enough: be careful with what you incentivize, pay attention to the results, and build a culture where dishonest or fraudulent behavior isn't tolerated. Unfortunately, that's not the lesson the bank learned. Instead, in a classic case of corporate overreaction, they eliminated their incentivization program entirely. Talk about using a tank to kill a fly.

This is why automating systems and adopting flashy tools isn't enough. Sure, an automated platform can save your organization from hours upon hours of rote work, but if you're not careful, all you're doing is making it easier to drive harmful behaviors.

This is why, at Xactly, we focus so heavily not on driving results, but on driving target behaviors. Incentivize based on the number of new accounts, and watch as your sales team finds increasingly dodgy ways to maximize the number of new accounts they open. Incentivize a behavior that *leads* to new accounts—such as reaching out to new leads—and you'll be far more likely to get the outcome you were actually targeting.

Feel free to get creative here. If you can dream it, and it's measurable, you can incentivize it. We work with one client, for instance, who runs their entire corporate bonus program by incentivizing target behaviors—an engineer completing an SES, a team reaching a group milestone, a lead-gen representative completing a set number of calls, and so on.

Another organization we work with incentivizes customer-facing behaviors—such as smiling, dressing appropriately, greeting people nicely, and so on. These may not sound like the most scientific of measures—and the organization may be hard-pressed to point to clear results from these behaviors—but because even actions like this can be measured and recorded, it still works.

This is all to say that the sky's the limit when incentivizing behavior in your Intelligent Revenue program. But however you approach it, make sure that your target behaviors are tied to clear revenue outcomes.

CASE STUDY: WORKIVA

Workiva is on a mission to power transparent reporting for a better world. Their cloud-based platform simplifies the most complex reporting and disclosure challenges by streamlining processes, connecting data and teams, and ensuring consistency.

Prior to working with Xactly, Workiva's compensation processes were managed manually. Everything tracked was linked to a different spreadsheet, which meant every part of the process was excessively complex, time consuming, and error prone. This manual process resulted in extensive time spent on manual calculations and shadow accounting.

This system was unsustainable and unscalable, and the Workiva team knew it. Needing a single solution to streamline sales compensation processes and dataflows, Workiva adopted an Intelligent Revenue approach to both net some quick wins and position their revenue operation for the future.

By implementing a centralized, real-time view of its sales performance and compensation data, Workiva now saves time and reduces errors in its compensation processes. Sales reps can track their individual performance against their plan and commission earnings, while the admins can track plan effectiveness through detailed performance versus pay data analytics.

The effects on their sales operation have been unmistakable. Since partnering with Xactly, Workiva has seen the following:

- Ninety-nine percent reduction in post-payroll processing spend
- Ninety-five percent reduction in disputes and time to resolve tickets (from thirty-plus days to fewer than three)
- Ninety-five percent reduction in service-level agreement (SLA) turnaround (from thirty-plus days to fewer than three)
- Improved bookings and data integrity
- Simplified accrual efforts and reconciliation process
- Increased visibility for executives, RevOps, and compensation team
- Added flexibility for Workiva's compensation plan design

More important than the numbers, however, is the effect these changes have had on the sales team's morale. Sellers no longer worry about the accuracy of their compensation and how they're paid. They know it's right. Without having to spend all that time shadow accounting, they have extra time each week to focus on what they do best: selling.

With reps and admins no longer focusing on manually managing compensation processes, they can now focus on creating greater impact by improving collaboration and performance. Workiva is able to set firmer sales stage definitions, review deal health scores, and take action on activity alerts to improve that scoring.

Do that, and you'll be one step closer to building an incentivization program that benefits both your company and your sales team. And from there, you're one step closer to implementing a sales culture that will allow you to reach your loftiest goals.

INTELLIGENT REVENUE TUNE-UPS

→ How many adjustments has your comp team done in the last month? What is the average turnover of your salespeople?

→ How many measures are on your comp plan? Is that number greater than five, greater than ten, or even greater than fifteen?

→ Do you think your sales plans are in alignment with your CEO's desires? Is shadow accounting harming productivity and trust?

→ What recordable metrics can you target and incentivize that will lead to positive change?

CHAPTER 6

STOP BEING A ONE-TRICK PONY

WHEN YOU THINK OF A BRAND LIKE PENNZOIL-QUAKER State, what do you think of?

Probably motor oil—which is exactly what their sales reps thought too. That's all they sold. They made their quotas on oil. They hit their multipliers on oil. They made the president's club on oil. So oil was all that mattered.

Of course, oil was not the only product that Pennzoil-Quaker State sold. They had eight different product families—including air fresheners, tire cleaners, oil filters, and so on. By no means did their CEO want his reps to *stop* selling oil, but he didn't want them hitting all their incentives on oil alone, especially when they had more profitable products.

So we made a change to the sales team's compensation plan, adding product gates so that their reps couldn't hit all their numbers on oil alone. To get those multipliers or make the president's club, they had to sell a minimum amount of items from every product family.

Lo and behold, seemingly overnight, that's exactly what their sales reps did.

As a result, Pennzoil-Quaker State's sales function went from being a one-trick pony to a dynamic revenue operation that targeted a balanced product mix that positioned them for long-term success.

Would-be unicorns don't care where their sales come from. They only care about instant growth. Often, this results in a limited product mix and an emphasis on products that drive short-term revenue at the expense of better margins or predictable revenue. To create a better product balance, sales leaders must learn to identify and incentivize target behaviors within their sales team. In this chapter, we'll explore how.

SALES DOESN'T HAVE TO BE COIN OPERATED

You've probably heard the old saying that all sales reps are coin operated. It's natural for a sales rep to want to seek out the biggest payday for themselves. However, if we assume that's all that motivates a person, then we risk ignoring some other basic human motivators.

People want connections beyond money—yes, even sales reps. They want to understand how what they do in their area impacts the bigger picture. They want to feel like they're contributing to a better world.

Part of that means incentivizing sales reps to value quality revenue that's sustainable and diverse. It's difficult to focus on making a positive impact when your company is fighting to stay above water. If your sales reps make this connection, they're likely to assist with your mission, bypassing easy deals for more profitable options.

Sales leaders following an Intelligent Revenue framework

can help their sales reps embrace diversification. In fact, it's in their best interests to do so.

No business is static. Sometimes, due to changes in the market, changes in the product mix, or changes in buyer behavior, you have to shift your sales strategy. For instance, your sales operation might need to change tactics from a relationship-based sales approach to a solution-oriented approach.

Certainly, this is a manageable change. However, it does require a shift in behavior on the part of your sales reps, who now must have a much deeper understanding of their customers' business and challenges.

Hiring alone won't enable that shift in your sales team. After all, the market is seemingly always tight for skilled salespeople. To shift successfully, you will need to develop from within at the same time you hire from outside. If you can learn how to incentivize your sales team, you can help drive this behavior change.

Following an Intelligent Revenue approach, the sales leader's job is threefold:

1. **Create the right system of incentives.** Initiatives like the "Rule of X" can lead to a better balance of predictable revenue and diverse revenue streams. This is a long-term strategy that targets and reinforces the sales behaviors you're looking for.

2. **Use available data to demonstrate that the kinds of deals you're incentivizing are not just attainable, but desirable.** Here, proof of concept is everything. If someone else has done it, they can too. Most sales reps aren't lacking in self-confidence and competitiveness. As soon as you show them what they can do, they'll do it.

3. **Set up your reps to succeed.** Points one and two are nothing if your reps don't believe they are set up to succeed. Do

they have enough deals in their territory? Is their quota appropriate and beatable? Given unrealistic goals or a lack of opportunity, people will leave. The better you can demonstrate that every sales rep has an equal opportunity, the better they will feel about putting in their best effort.

These are the most crucial factors in designing a compensation plan that incentivizes the right kinds of performance. Proving that targets are attainable and giving people the tools they need to succeed will prompt them to pursue the incentives and drive quality revenue. Then, with that data-based plan, you can predict results, make adjustments, and backfill deals to hit your number. The company succeeds and your reps flourish. From there, the key is simply to incentivize the right behaviors.

RETHINKING SYSTEMS AND INCENTIVES

Thought leader Daniel Pink is a known critic of incentive-based systems. From his perspective, incentivization only works when the task at hand is cognitively simple.

In principle, I agree with this argument. After all, if I put ten people in a room and said I'd pay each of them a million dollars if they could come up with the next Google or Amazon, it's probably not going to work. Sure, that's a big incentive. And sure, it'll likely motivate the people in that room to at least try. But that money isn't necessarily going to allow anyone to think more creatively. In fact, with such tremendous pressure on them, it might end up doing the opposite.

However, where Pink and I differ is our perception of the sales function. He sees sales as fundamentally too complex for an incentive system to work. I say that sales is really as simple as it seems—and that a good compensation plan is even simpler.

If you were on your first day as a salesperson and I told you that I would pay $50 extra for every red bike you sold, is there any question what you would do next? Simple incentives drive simple behaviors. And for the several million salespeople who exist in the world, it really is that basic.

But not only that, it's also important. You cannot have Intelligent Revenue without at least a basic incentive system in place. Without it, your sales team will just sell whatever is easiest for them to sell. And while you could argue that some revenue is better than no revenue, I disagree. If those sales aren't helping you to reach your goals, then that revenue is essentially meaningless.

The obstacle, then, is proper incentivization. One of the common challenges of incentivization has always been the imbalance between carrot and stick. In the traditional model, the stick (the spreadsheet) was too weak, and the carrot (the incentive structure) was too big. The second a revenue operation wanted to drive a specific behavior, the spreadsheet would break under the weight of trying to support a complex compensation plan. Intelligent Revenue solves this problem by creating a more sophisticated carrot and stick.

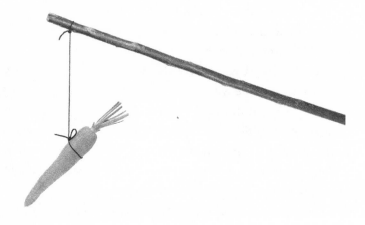

We've all seen the image of the dangling carrot. Usually, somebody is sitting atop an animal that, for whatever reason, refuses to budge. So the person attaches a carrot to a line of string, attaches it to a stick, and hangs it in front of the animal's face. Motivated by the treat, the animal begins to move.

Sales leaders love to think of all the different carrots they can add in when planning out their compensation structure. It's a great idea, but there's just one problem: they forget to *dangle* that carrot.

In a typical company, the sales compensation system is somewhat opaque. As a salesperson, you close the deal, the finance team does their magic on a spreadsheet somewhere, and then they send you a report telling you how much you made on that sale.

That's all well and good—at least you're getting paid. But if you don't know what incentives kicked in, how you got to that number, how much you *could* have made by modifying your offer, or what to sell in order to earn the highest compensation, then none of those incentives really matter. Your focus is simply on selling what you can and getting paid.

To show what I mean, imagine you're selling bicycles, and you're working with a potential buyer on a custom quote. Step by step, you walk them through the selection process. Do you want a three-, five-, or ten-speed? Do you want a red frame or a blue frame?

As the salesperson, you know that if you sell a bike in any configuration, you're getting paid. But you may not know how much more you could be paid by selling a *specific* configuration. Imagine if, as you're on the phone with your prospective buyer, the system told you there was a spif (short for *sales program incentive fund*) for all red-framed bikes, since your warehouse is sitting on a big stockpile. For each red-framed bike you sell, you'll get 150 percent of the payout that you would have received for a blue-framed bike.

That's what dangling the carrot is meant to be about: changing behavior. Too many comp systems make it too difficult for the salesperson to understand where their escalators are and how to trigger them. Meanwhile, that stockpile of red frames in your warehouse isn't getting any smaller. A spreadsheet can't affect behavior in real time—but a cloud-based system with built-in prompts and calculators can.

A STRONGER STICK

Ninety-nine times out of a hundred, the results the CEO wants to see and the behaviors the comp plan incentivizes couldn't be further apart. The CEO wants to sell their massive stockpile of red bike frames, and the comp plan only incentivizes sales volume.

The primary culprit? Comp plans are hard as hell to track on a spreadsheet. It's cumbersome to update, it's prone to human error, and it's not built for real-time adjustments. Often, the plan has to be dumbed down from what the CEO wants in order to drive *any* behavior at all.

But when you can automate, when you can create a credible system that people can rely on, you get a whole slew of additional benefits:

- **Sudden shifts in direction.** Say your organization has a big product launch mid-quarter. An Intelligent Revenue approach could help to prioritize that launch by adding a spif (sales program incentive fund) to the campaign—say, a trip to Vegas for the first rep to sell ten of a certain product.
- **Time-savings take backs.** An automated system means you don't need a file manager to feed inputs into your spreadsheet; the inputs come directly from the source.
- **Accurate real-time reporting.** Reps can access the information on a real-time basis, which motivates them while also reducing incoming calls to the central administration team asking about their compensation. They can just look at the app. As a result, sales leaders find they can spend more time managing the actual pipeline, rather than putting out fires.
- **Greater transparency.** Reps can look at the dashboard any time they want and see how close they are to reaching their goal. That transparency drives performance, just like seeing your weight on a scale drives healthy behavior. Visibility makes the goal more real.

Again, it's not just about individual progress, but about how the organization is performing relative to its goals. Intelligent Revenue uses tools that allow sales reps a view not only of their individual performance, but of how the revenue operation is performing overall—including what parts of the go-to-market strategy need to adjust and whether the company is on track to make its number.

A HEALTHIER CARROT

Some organizations we work with spend as much as $2 billion on variable compensation a year. Whatever your own numbers, variable comp is surely one of your largest annual expenditures. As such, I'm sure your CFO would appreciate that you're leveraging this expenditure correctly—and that you're getting the results you want.

Let me be clear on this next point, because it's an important one.

Just because you can do more with an Intelligent Revenue framework *does not* mean you should build a more complicated comp plan.

Really. Better to use Intelligent Revenue to drive a few specific incentives successfully than to drive several incentives poorly.

Science, industry wisdom, and our own data all back this up: the more you try to measure, the less effective you'll be. The companies that pay out on only three—that's right, three—measures perform much better than those that pay out on six, seven, or eight measures or more.

Why is that? Take a hundred-dollar bill and divide it up ten ways. If you miss a couple of measures but hit all the other ones, you're not going to miss your target number by much. However, if you're only focused on three measures, then missing even one of them is going to have a considerable effect on your payout. To hit your numbers, you're going to focus on hitting all three of those measures.

Remember, it's hard to drive the behavior you want if your message isn't clear. The more complicated your comp plan, the more confusion you're going to create. The better your sales reps understand the plan, the more focused they will be in how they spend their time, what kinds of conversations they have, and what kinds of products they choose to sell.

To create a better carrot, then, your job is simple: determine the three measures that are most important to you and track them.

Gaming the plan means figuring out what you want to do and having your reps run after it. But they'll only run after it if they understand it—and how it benefits them. If the math is too complex and people don't see how the plan works, you're not leveraging the strategy. You're just creating confusion.

It might seem counterintuitive at first, but sometimes simple really is better. You don't need a complicated incentivization system to change behavior. You just need a good carrot and a good stick.

NOT EVERYONE WANTS A BIG-SCREEN TV

When I was a young sales leader with a young family, I had my heart set on getting a big-screen TV for our living room. What better way to bring your family together, right?

Inspired by my own want, I decided to run a spif for my sales team, with a big-screen TV as a bonus for reaching a big company goal. My reasoning was simple: If a big-screen TV had recently been a big motivator for me, then surely everyone else on my sales team would have the same priorities, right?

As it turned out, no. Not long after I announced the spif, one of my reps came up to me and said, "Chris, I don't need a big-screen TV. I already have one."

CASE STUDY: HIGHSPOT

Founded in 2012, Highspot is a software company employing over eight hundred people. When the COVID-19 pandemic hit and Highspot's sales team went remote, Highspot initially found it difficult to provide their sales reps with the coaching and resources they needed to thrive in their jobs.

To strengthen their relationship with their remote teams, Highspot focused on two things. First, Highspot wanted all their reps to understand how their compensation plans worked. To do that, they adopted Xactly's Incent tool, which not only added considerable transparency to the sales process with their dashboarding feature but also allowed their customer, John Garand of Highspot, to adapt his coaching style to a more remote environment.

Second, Highspot wanted their reps to focus their energy only on the deals with the highest earning potential. Once again, Xactly's Incent tool added clarity to the process and helped reps quickly identify the deals that would max out their compensation plans.

The result, as Highspot put it, was "a really great year." One rep even hit their annual on-target earnings in a single month. When the rest of the team saw how well this new system worked, they were all racing to duplicate the results of their top-earning sellers.

That stopped me dead in my tracks. How lame was it that I would dangle this carrot that at least one of my sales reps didn't even want to win? Not only was it de-motivating, it was a little myopic. Just because I thought something was really cool didn't mean that everyone on my team would think the same thing.

Contrast that story with the experience of a sales rep I once knew. One day, his sales manager came up to him and said, "Hey, if you close these three deals on your plate by the end of this quarter, what would you spend your commission money on?"

Without hesitation, the rep said that he would buy a Scotty Cameron putter, which he'd been eyeing for quite some time.

Over the course of the quarter, the rep forgot about the conversation. He just went about his business and worked to close those three deals—which he did. Finally, the end-of-the-quarter meeting rolled around, and to his surprise, his sales manager presented him with that Scotty Cameron putter.

The rep was floored. His manager had never directly incentivized him with the putter—or with anything, for that matter. He'd simply listened to the rep so that he could learn what motivated him and used that motivation to reward the right behavior.

THE RIGHT APPROACH SATISFIES EVERYONE

You can work toward Intelligent Revenue and keep your salespeople happy and productive. In fact, there's no other way. It takes everyone working in proper alignment to create a quality revenue operation.

Figure out what drives your people, and use that knowledge to incentivize behaviors your company deems necessary for long-term success. But incentives are like diminishing returns. More might seem better, but each new incentive you introduce into your comp plan devalues the rest. Stick to three so that reps care deeply about each of them.

A straightforward comp plan aids transparency. Incentives are no good if reps don't know about them or understand how they work. Remember, how you dangle the carrot is just as important as the carrot itself. The proper tools allow you to do this in real time.

Bad revenue is the same as no revenue. That's why the unicorn approach has been effectively replaced by quality revenue. Growth is meaningless if it isn't done the right way. Following that thread, what your reps are selling is just as important as how much they're selling. A diverse product mix provides repeatable, predictable revenue. Your company should never be reliant on one source of revenue. That's a recipe for disaster.

Those same Intelligent Revenue solutions that help us know what to sell and how to incentivize sales reps have another critical responsibility: predicting the future. The confidence with which you're able to do this can make all the difference when it comes to achieving your goals.

INTELLIGENT REVENUE = INTELLIGENT LEADERSHIP

In Chapter 4, we talked about the many problems of running your revenue operations on spreadsheets. Here's one I left out: a sales leader's ability to effectively lead their reps. Why? Because spreadsheets dumb down comp plans into a one-size-fits-all model that—surprise, surprise—may not actually fit your sales organization at all.

Get to know the people that you're leading. Everybody has different things that make them tick. All you have to do is ask questions. For example:

- If a given salesperson is closing a deal, what are they going to do with that commission money?
- How focused are your team members on work–life balance or balancing their responsibilities to their families?
- How do your sales reps envision performance translating into opportunities for growth at your company?

In an Intelligent Revenue model using modern tools you can customize your comp plans so that they account for what actually motivates your sales reps. And if the aspects that motivate certain branches of your sales team are different than others, no problem; you can work those interdepartmental differences in there too.

INTELLIGENT REVENUE TUNE-UPS

→ Is your comp plan clear enough to drive the sales objectives your leadership is looking for?

→ Do you know what incentivizes your sales reps? What are their top priorities in career and life?

→ How does your product mix lend itself to a quality revenue operation? Is your company a one-trick pony?

CHAPTER 7

DITCH THE HERO CULTURE

IMAGINE YOU'RE A FIRST-LINE SALES MANAGER WITH TEN reps working for you.

Of those ten reps, you have three top performers, three who are either terrible or just getting started (they don't even know where the bathroom is), and three in the middle who are...okay.

When the Glengarry leads come in—the most substantive, lucrative leads—who are you going to give them to?

That's right: one of your three top performers. These are the deals you can't afford to screw up—and you *know* your top performers will close on them ninety-nine times out of a hundred. You trust them completely.

I remember following this same approach when I was a sales leader—and to good results. The problem, though, is that you don't just do this once, but all the time. It's an ongoing business strategy, and it's adversely affecting the quality of your sales team.

By always going with the sure hands, you're perpetuating

a toxic hero culture that is destroying the morale of your sales operation. Sure, the best horses in your stable are getting their reps in, but what about everyone else? They're still waiting in their stalls not making any money.

And they're pissed.

Once you're aware of the issue, however, you should make it your top priority to break that cycle. Instead of designing a system where your workhorses are always getting the premium leads, ask how you can create more balanced territories so that everyone gets equal opportunities.

With the right tools and technology, you can balance things such that you could place your territories on a dartboard, line up each rep, and tell them that whatever they hit is theirs. And because each slice of the dartboard has equal value, they'll be happy to play the game. This isn't something that most sales operations are capable of doing today—and yet the technology already exists for them to do it.

Wouldn't a balanced approach set up your sales operation for more long-term continuity and growth? This is a key piece of Intelligent Revenue and a great way to make your sales team more productive.

Sales organizations that rely on a single rock star sales leader—or a small group of all-star performers—may see short-term success, but ultimately this model is unsustainable.

Better yet, what if everyone in your sales operation could become a high performer? To get there, we have to get to the bottom of what's causing this reliance on what we refer to as "hero culture."

THE BIMODAL PERFORMER PROBLEM

In any organization, especially in any sales operation, you can usually divide your employees into three tiers: top performers, average or mediocre performers, and poor performers.

In a typical organization, you would expect your performers to fall out along a standard bell curve—with some people overperforming, some people underperforming, and the rest in the middle.

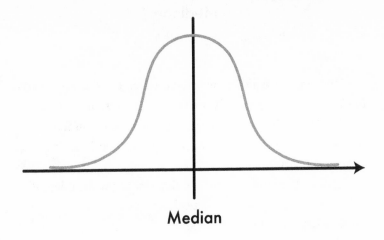

Median

If you assume that your team's performance mirrors a standard distribution, I understand why you might think that, but I've got some bad news for you. At most organizations today, we're seeing their sales reps perform something like this:

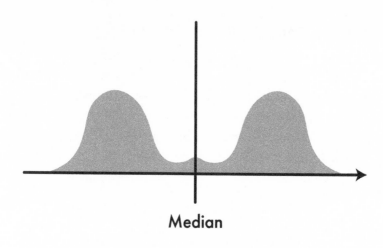

Median

This ugly-looking fellow is what we call a *bimodal distribution curve*. In terms of your sales organization, this shows you've got a problem—specifically, an outsized amount of both top performers (yay!) and poor performers (boo!), but little to no average performers.

In case there's any confusion, that's not how the talent distribution should look in a healthy business.

So what's causing this problem?

I'll be honest: the jury is still out. Our research lab has spent a lot of time looking into this, and we've yet to come up with a single answer. Most likely, it's a combination of factors—the biggest of which we refer to as *the Silver Medalist Effect*.

NOT A PERFORMANCE PROBLEM, BUT A PEOPLE PROBLEM

In 2017, we wanted to look deeper into the nature of attrition in today's organizations—not just how many people were leaving, but *who* was leaving. To do that, our research team took a large dataset charting hires and attritions in sales operations for the year. In our dataset, we had over twenty-seven thousand new hires and roughly sixteen thousand attritions. Our researchers then took this dataset and separated employees into different bands based on performance.

The results floored us. Across all different bands, the group that had the highest attrition rate—at three times the rate for the rest of the sales team—was the second-tier performers. Not the top performers, but still valuable, tough-to-replace players in any organization. And while these second-tier performers fled their organizations, guess who stuck around? That's right: the third- and fourth-tier players.

Think of those third-tier performers like the average to below-average segment of a sales force, and the fourth-tier as performing well below standards. Some of the third-tier is undoubtedly useful, but these two groups as a whole aren't taking your organization where it needs to go—and they certainly aren't driving a shift to Intelligent Revenue.

Why was this happening?

Chalk it up to something called the *Silver Medalist Effect*. First described in 1995 by researchers V. H. Medvec, S. F. Madey, and T. Gilovich, the Silver Medalist Effect has been used to describe a particular phenomenon among the top three people to reach the podium—gold, silver, and bronze medalists—in competitive sports.

Here's how the phenomenon goes. When you win gold, you're happy. You're on top of the world. When you win bronze, sure, it may only be third place, but you're just happy to make the podium. Gold is out of reach, thus, you don't feel like you missed out. When you win silver, however, you're angry. Why? Because only a single person stands between you and victory. You're so close you can taste it, and yet someone still stands in your way.[19] Now, in terms of our study, we can't prove that all your silver medalist reps leave because they're unhappy. But with data-driven intelligence, we *can* prove that they're more likely to leave. And who can blame them? Stay with their current company, and they're blocked from landing all the Glengarry leads by other top performers. But at another company, they'll have more opportunities to take the top spot on the podium.

The question is, what are you going to do with that information? I know what I'd do. I'd pull up the database for my sales reps, identify all my silver medalists, and start checking in with them to find out how they're doing. After all, it's either that, or sit back and watch as some of my most reliable performers leave.

There's nothing wrong with having a small stable of absolute rock stars in your sales force. We have our own rock stars, and we know exactly who they are. However, rely too heavily on those rock stars, and you'll find it difficult to scale your revenue operation. After all, when 80 percent of the results come from just 20 percent of your sales team, throwing more bodies onto your team isn't likely to move the needle for you very much. Rock star performers don't just grow on trees, you know.

In fact, they're in incredibly high demand. You're more likely to *lose* some of your top performers than attract new ones. According to a 2022 study commissioned by Xactly, 85 percent of senior sales professionals were planning to change their jobs if the US economy didn't improve.[20] The numbers aren't much

---

19 V. H. Medvec, S. F. Madey, and T. Gilovich, "When Less Is More: Counterfactual Thinking and Satisfaction Among Olympic Medalists," *Journal of Personality and Social Psychology* 69, no. 4 (1995): 603–10, https://doi.org/10.1037//0022-3514.69.4.603; Vanessa Romo, "Why Bronze Medalists Are Likely Happier Than Those Who Win Silver," NPR, July 29, 2021, https://www.npr.org/2021/07/29/1022537817/theres-a-psychology-lesson-behind-why-olympic-bronze-medalists-are-so-happy.

20 Cloey Callahan, "Why Companies Are Worrying Over Potentially High Sales Exec Exits," WorkLife, September 15, 2022, https://www.worklife.news/talent/sales-talent-crisis/.

more encouraging for rank-and-file sales professionals either. A 2021 Xactly study found a 58 percent increase in attrition among sales professionals from the previous year.[21]

Let's put this all together:

- Your top performers are at risk of leaving (or being poached) for greener pastures.
- Your silver medalists are at risk of leaving because they don't feel like they have a fair opportunity at your company.
- Your bottom-tier players are happy to stay put. After all, if you haven't noticed they're not pulling their weight yet, then when will you?

So what can you do? We'll explore more culture-centric ways to stop attrition in the next chapter. For the rest of this chapter, we're going to focus on how to level the playing field by improving your sales planning and go-to-market strategies. When everyone is performing to the best extent possible, you won't have to rely on a few rock stars because you're setting everyone up to succeed.

TAKE THE ASSUMPTIONS OUT OF PLANNING

Every organization wants to achieve a competitive advantage. Those who plan with the most accuracy have the best chance of doing so. I'm going to take a guess about what the planning process for your organization's go-to-market strategy looks like.

At the end of the year, you sit down to map out what you

---

21 Xactly, "The Sales Talent Crisis: Xactly Releases Data on Sales Team Turnover and Retention Insights," press release, September 13, 2022, https://www.xactlycorp.com/company/press-room/sales-talent-crisis-xactly-releases-data-sales-team-turnover-and-retention.

expect the year ahead to look like. To do that, you make a series of assumptions:

- How many reps you'll hire and onboard, and on what schedule
- How soon they will close their first deal
- What the ramp-up process toward new-hire productivity looks like
- What their average deal size, discount, and performance will be
- What the attrition rate is and how fast you plan to replace attrition (one of the biggest hindrances to any sales plan is the failure to hire reps fast enough to replace those who leave)

And on it goes, assumption after assumption. Sure, they're informed assumptions, but they're still assumptions all the same.

You can tell just by looking at this approach that it's got more holes in it than a slice of Swiss cheese. Inaccuracies, after all, compound like interest—and an assumption-based approach leaves *a lot* of room for inaccuracies.

Nevertheless, sales and finance leaders persist with this approach, mostly because they don't think they have any choice. They use their manual tools because that's all they know. They don't have the tools, systems, or data to do it any other way. And so they accept the devil they know and the imperfect results it produces. The CRO synthesizes these estimates, the CFO establishes a plan for business, and the board approves a budget to fund the go-to-market strategy for the sales team.

And then, having fulfilled its purpose, that assumption-riddled sales plan sits in a drawer for the rest of the year. It's the basis for all numbers, quotas, and hiring plans, but no one ever bothers to pull it back out and check its validity. The sales plan never gets updated based on how things are actually progressing.

This approach may have worked just fine fifty years ago, but it doesn't now. In fact, it creates two big problems. First, there's the issue of permanence. Why in the world would you want a one-and-done plan? Why wouldn't you want something that lives and breathes and changes? As Mike Tyson once famously said, "Everyone has a plan until they get punched in the mouth." Right out of the gate, two weeks after budget approval, conditions might change and require you to modify the entire plan.

If you're stuck in the old way of doing things, you won't. You'll stick with the original plan, come hell or high water. If you have a *living plan* that can be updated in real time, then you can prevent your sales operation from going too far down the wrong path.

This brings us to our second point. A fixed plan lives and dies by its assumptions—which is, as I've already alluded to, about as solid as a slice of Swiss cheese. How do you plan effectively without having reliable, real-time data? You don't. But with a living plan, you can track actual performance against all the assumptions you made throughout the year.

"But, Chris," you say, "I do have reliable data. I have last year's numbers as a benchmark."

True—that *is* data. But it's not the kind of data that can help you make any kind of informed decision. For instance, say your company has reviewed the past year's performance and decides it wants to grow by 40 percent year over year. Sounds like a reasonable goal, but is it?

Hard to say. The only real indicators you have to go by are last year's earnings and maybe some industry benchmarks that your finance team pulled together. These benchmarks might appear better than nothing, but in reality they're a shot in the dark. Do these numbers from other companies in other sectors *really* align with what's happening in your own business? Again, without the proper data from your own company, how can you know? You can't. You're planning in a vacuum—and assuming you're on the right path.

Here's where the problem compounds. Once your organization has set its sights on 40 percent growth, it figures there's only one good way to do it: increase sales capacity. Now, this approach can absolutely work, but is it the only way? Is it *the best way*?

These are the kinds of questions someone following an Intelligent Revenue framework would ask as they seek to not only increase revenue, but to increase quality of revenue. As it turns out, there are a lot of different ways to build your go-to-market strategy—and not all of them are created equal.

That's why it's so important to get your sales planning right. Following an Intelligent Revenue approach, planning is a lot more than a simple numbers exercise that gets stuffed in a drawer. It's a dynamic, data-based, and adaptable approach that allows your revenue operation to develop a more comprehensive and effective go-to-market strategy.

It's not only possible but necessary to use automation in a way that increases planning accuracy and relies less on assumptions. We can utilize predictive modeling to create estimates and update in real time. Based on previous performance and success, automation quantifies existing demand and forms a plan to capture the maximum amount.

Like we touched on in Chapter 4, all of this serves to establish a positive feedback loop. De-siloing and fully integrating between your organization's systems is the most thorough and efficient way to make use of data.

ESTABLISH BETTER BENCHMARKS

One year, our finance team was convinced we should set our sales number to $100 million. Reaching that number was easy, they said. All our sales reps would have to do was hit an average of 80 percent of their quotas. Almost as an afterthought, they added, "Of course, that number is very hot."

This stopped me in my tracks. "Why?" I asked.

As they explained, another similar company had needed their reps to perform at only 70 percent to hit their number, so our 80 percent number implied that we had to be a little more on top of our game.

At first blush, this sounded like a reasonable conclusion. But on closer inspection, there were a lot of unknowns. What was the company's average quota, and how did ours compare? Were ours artificially lower? If so, of course our plan would necessitate our sales team to perform at a higher percentage.

In this case, by asking some basic questions, we determined that external benchmarking alone wasn't enough to base our decision on. Without more context, the data simply wasn't helpful. Instead, all I wanted to see was how much revenue per head we needed in order to reach $100 million, and how that number compared to our revenue per head from the previous year.

In this situation, I knew that comparison would be a more meaningful way to vet whether that $100 million sales goal was realistic. In other contexts, I might have sought out other tributaries to improve quality revenue, such as improving churn, adding price increases, upselling, prioritizing new products, and so on.

In an Intelligent Revenue framework, "sell more" is just one of the levers you can pull, and your benchmarks should reflect that. Instead of just trotting out numbers to compare your own business against, you're more concerned with making sure you're looking at the question from the right perspective. After all, a different lens can lead to a totally different conclusion, so it's essential to have legitimate, accurate benchmarks and then apply them using your leadership expertise.

I know what you're thinking: Easier said than done, right?

Sure. Businesses often encounter several problems when it comes to benchmarking.

First is a lack of data. You can't know if you're beautiful or ugly if you've never looked in a mirror or you've never seen another human. You have nothing to compare yourself to. Similarly, if you don't have the data to benchmark, then you don't know where your company stands with regard to your competitors and your potential.

Second is too much data—or at least, a big data pool with a lot of uncertainty on how to use it. How can you know when to compare your plans against your own numbers, when to compare them against your competitors, or when to do a combination of both?

Benchmarking requires understanding where you are, what your trajectory is, and how others in your industry are performing. Only through accurate data analysis can you determine whether you're setting the bar too high or too low. Let's look at a few applications to shed some further light on the subject.

CREATE A BETTER RAMP-UP PLAN

Time matters. Getting your sales reps up to speed in a timely manner can be the difference between a competitive advantage or falling behind the competition.

How long do your reps take to ramp up to 100 percent of quota? How long does it take them to fully learn their product, their territory, or their company?

Three months? Six months? Ten months?

Do you actually know, or are you going off an assumption?

For most sales VPs, it's the latter. Sure, it might feel like your reps are just about up to speed after being on the floor for six months, but if the reality is more like nine to twelve months, that difference is going to dramatically throw off your sales plan.

But here's another question: How does your average ramp-up time compare to similar organizations? Are your reps ahead of the curve, right on it, or well behind it? What does the curve even look like?

Thanks to nearly twenty years of objective data, we actually know the answer. We've learned that, across the thousands of organizations we've worked with, the average ramp-up time for a sales rep at a small-to-midsize business (SMB) is 43.2 days. Meanwhile, the ramp-up time for a typical enterprise rep is much longer, between six and ten months.

A sales leader following an Intelligent Revenue model doesn't simply assume their ramp-up time is three months and then build their sales plan around that number. That's the epitome of paving the cow path. This assumption may seem useful, but ultimately it's counterproductive.

With every assumption, the key is to ask (1) whether it's accurate and (2) whether that number can be improved. Then, using modern sales planning tools, you can generate accurate plans that account for your reps' ramp-up time—thereby maximizing the value of each rep.

It's one thing to think that a nine-month ramp-up for your reps is fine when you don't have the data. However, as soon as you can see that the industry average is six and you do nothing about it, shame on you. That's ridiculous. How could you possibly be okay with your system being so inefficient that it takes a whole additional quarter to figure out how to close a deal?

Following an Intelligent Revenue perspective, the second a sales leader saw that their organization was wildly trailing the average in terms of ramp-up time, they would investigate to find the source of the problem. The problem could be any number of factors, including lead generation, sales, recruiting, onboarding, and training. The exact answer would depend on the details of your situation, but the data helps you know where to look.

Without robust benchmarking data, however, you wouldn't be able to do any of this. It would all be a guessing game—just you and your team randomly tinkering with hundreds of interconnected moving parts because you have no idea where to start. With the data, you have a much better idea of where to investigate.

Then once you've identified the issue, you have a better path to predictability. It's perfectly reasonable to expect that new hires will have a nonproductive first quarter while they learn the ropes ahead of closing their first deal. But if the data tells you they should be performing by the end of the second quarter, that knowledge allows you to plan better, make your decision-making more intelligent, and create a virtuous cycle around your ramp-ups.

Once a sales rep is up to speed, then comes the next phase of the game—their territory.

STEP UP YOUR TERRITORY GAME

Territories used to be about zip codes and how far you could travel. All that's gone away.

Sales reps can work from anywhere now. As long as there's a telephone line, a reliable internet connection, and an employee able to work responsibly without direct supervision, then that work can get done in any location.

Well, perhaps not any location. I do still think time zone matters—and depending on what industry you're in, it may be important that your reps *do* actually live in their local geographies. In other words, even if you're not in an industry where your sales team must live in the same zip code as their territory, it's still much easier for a rep from Washington State to contact a lead in California than it is for a rep in Washington, DC, to do the same thing.

Still, the bottom line in a post-COVID world is that you're no longer geographically bound when setting territories. The world has changed. If you're still doing things the old way, shame on you.

Always giving your best reps the most lucrative leads ties into this outdated model. You can't do things the way you used to and expect to improve revenue quality.

At its core, you have a territory problem. Every time you hand out the Glengarry leads, you create more imbalanced territories—and your reps know it. Often, when you hear an underperforming rep complain that Susie has a better territory or that Johnny gets the best deals because he's related to the CEO, listen to them. They have their reasons all mixed up, but they're at least partially right—and this confusion is a major contributor to the problem of bimodal curves that we discussed earlier.

Feedback like this is a clear sign that your sales reps aren't happy, which may foreshadow things to come. After all, unhappiness quickly compounds in an organization, which can have a big impact on your operation.

Do you know the top two reasons most sales reps leave their jobs?

1. They don't believe they're getting paid accurately.
2. They don't believe their territories are fair.

We've talked a lot about the first point already. Countless sales reps have been lost to needless shadow accounting due to the flaws of a manual comp system.

The second point, though, is a silent killer. And as the Great Resignation of 2021 and 2022 has shown us, people are more willing than ever to leave a job if they don't feel like they're being treated fairly.

Oftentimes a sales leader will rely on gut feeling to divide territories for their sales reps. The problem, of course, is that this gut feeling isn't based on objective data. The sales leader may believe that Silicon Valley is a "rich patch" and Cincinnati is a "bad patch," but that belief is based on circumstantial evidence. What if Cincinnati was a potential gold mine and the company was missing out on millions of dollars in potential revenue simply because the sales leader wasn't assigning good reps to the territory? Without a data-based approach, neither the sales leader nor the company would ever know.

If you approach your territory planning in a similar way, I get it. That's the way it's always been done, and you've likely seen *some* positive results from this approach. But here's my question to you: What opportunities might you be missing? What opportunities are you denying your reps simply because you don't know about them? How much money are you leaving on the table?

Hunches, limited data, and assumptions just aren't smart enough, even when you have relatively experienced, knowledgeable people working on a problem. They need the right tools.

An Intelligent Revenue approach relies on data and machine learning to set equitable territories free from assumptions and favoritism. This approach offers sales leaders several benefits:

- When a sales rep's performance falters in a given territory, it is much easier to discern why and develop a productive response.
- If a rep has an issue with their territory, you can transparently show how it was calculated and why all the territories are fair and give reps an equal shot.
- You have a clearer picture of your total addressable market (TAM)—in other words, your untapped potential buyers.

This last item could have a significant impact on your future revenue. Sales operations still in the Stone Age look at TAM in fairly basic terms. They'll look at a sales rep and say, "Tom, you're a product specialist for this product, so your territory is Kansas."

Who knows, maybe Tom will absolutely kill it in Kansas. But without clear data, without a sense of the TAM, it's a crapshoot whether Kansas will pay off more than, say, Nebraska. There could be a significant opportunity in Kansas, or there could be very little. For Tom, that roll of the dice hardly seems fair.

An Intelligent Revenue approach can help you tease out the data to determine which territories have the greatest opportunities to make better decisions around those assignments.

For example, imagine that you have 1,200 customers, the majority of whom use your flagship product (Product A), but not your supporting tool (Product B). IR tools can create an internal TAM that forecasts what it would be worth to sell Product B to every one of your existing customers. Then it could create equitable territories for Product B that are filled with potential buyers.

Of course, there are other ways to slice the pie. Other datasets you can use to create fairer territories include these:

- Geography
- Ideal customer profile
- Pipeline data
- Market segmentation
- Customer data
- Sales potential for each area
- Distribution of the existing customer base
- Sales team size, goals, and expertise
- Travel and logistics
- Competitive landscape

Whatever the criteria, this level of specificity is all but impossible in a manual process, but is only a matter of a few keystrokes with the help of automation.

This advanced territory planning has additional benefits for the many sales reps who still have to physically travel from account to account within their territory. After all, the geographical characteristics of a region can dramatically impact results. How does a sales leader figure out the right territory for a rep, given personality, weather conditions, driving conditions, and so on? Again, tools exist to figure out those answers for you, accounting for drive times (among other variables) to ensure a rep can get everywhere they need to go.

UP-LEVEL YOUR SALES LEADERSHIP

There's this funny thing that happens in sales, where everyone in the company always seems to have an idea for how sales could improve their operation. "Sales should do X." "Sales should do Y." But put the shoe on the other foot. Imagine if your CRO went over to product and said, "Hey, can you build out this new app for me in a day?"

Product would look at that CRO like they were crazy. And yet, that's exactly the kind of request that CROs are asked to deal with day in and day out.

CROs have a tough job and would probably benefit from a more realistic set of expectations. Not only do you have to make numbers, but many have to make those numbers in an app-heavy environment where the tools don't always talk to each other—and at least half don't do anything valuable at all. How can you not be frustrated by that? Talk about a waste of energy.

My sense is that CROs would love it if they could condense their app ecosystem to a few core pieces that help drive business. This would help get the revenue operation's focus down to a few core elements.

The business world has changed in the past few years, which has only served to make the jobs of sales leaders more stressful. Deals are taking longer to close. As a leader, it's important that you lift up your reps so they don't get into the frustration of the weeds of sales.

Before the move to remote work happened (see Chapter 9), sales leaders could do this relatively easily by walking the floor and having impromptu discussions. There was also a sense of group stakes and dynamics; when someone landed a sale, they'd ring a large bell so that everyone knew—and then wanted to go find a deal of their own.

This isn't to say that you can't still bring an element of that environment to the remote workplace. At Xactly, we've found a way to ring the bell digitally so that our sales reps still feel some of that camaraderie and motivation to drive their own results. Even if you're working remotely, these kinds of things are still important.

The changes go beyond oversight and motivation techniques. Now, modern sales leaders are getting much more sophisticated. They understand that the future of sales and marketing is much more technical, and they understand the technology from a much more detailed and nuanced perspective than previous generations. They're happy to use tools. But because they know what these tools can do—and more importantly, what they *can't* do—they're becoming increasingly unwilling to waste their time on dead-end pseudo-fixes that someone from operations thought might help them.

Spending a fortune on tools that don't help you do a smarter job isn't the answer. In that same vein, there's far more to an organization's sales culture than money.

MONEY ISN'T THE ISSUE

Of all the reasons the sales leaders we surveyed gave for why they were leaving the company, money wasn't even on the list. Ahead of money were these:

- Work–life balance (20 percent)
- Lack of career opportunities (18 percent)
- Company culture (15 percent)
- Poor management (15 percent)
- Stress or burnout (12 percent)[22]

Granted, this study only focused on sales leaders—and the dirty little secret about sales leadership is that you actually make less than you probably did as a top-performing rep. These are people who were already willing to sacrifice the almighty dollar in favor of having greater influence and thought leadership.

Still, the data pointed to a trend. Yes, money is important,

---

22 Xactly, "The Sales Talent Crisis."

but it's not the be-all, end-all for why someone would stick with a job or seek another opportunity elsewhere. Our survey found that two-thirds of sales leaders would leave their job for another one that provides more purpose or value to society, and that nearly the same amount would take a pay cut to pursue

CASE STUDY: LINKEDIN

The bigger your revenue operation gets, the more difficult it is to perform strategic sales planning with accuracy and confidence, and manually managing every individual sales rep's compensation becomes untenable. Sure, when you're a big player like LinkedIn, you can afford someone on the finance team who spends their days calculating every single payout. But such work is neither necessary nor especially accurate—and it certainly doesn't take your company where you want to go.

As a continually evolving global company, LinkedIn needed a more reliable Intelligent Revenue solution that could help them reinvent themselves on the revenue operations side at the same pace as on the product side. To do that, they needed a tool set and a system that would allow them to increase efficiency for their sales operations and sales compensation teams, provide visibility into sales team targets and performance for their executives, and allow leaders to make quick and meaningful changes to sales plans that would drive the necessary sales behavior.

From this implementation, LinkedIn was able to grow their sales operation from 125 reps to five thousand over a ten-year period. This massive growth was only possible because the company knew they could rely on transparent, reliable, and easy-to-access data. A weekly tiger team made up of sales, HR, compensation, and finance helps drive sales planning and configure pay.

The result: better control and incredible efficiency. With the right systems in place, the LinkedIn team is able to be flexible and try new things without taking shots in the dark or disrupting their whole operation. Even in a year where the company had to change rules and plans three times more than usual, they were able to incorporate those changes seamlessly into their system.

more meaningful work.[23] Dangling a financial carrot when all your head of sales wants is a greater sense of purpose, in other words, is not going to work out. If you're not paying attention to how the world is changing and what your rock stars value, then you're going to lose some great people.

Actually, I'll amend that. Even if you *are* paying attention, you're still going to lose some great people. That's just the nature of the modern economy.

But you can minimize this risk simply by asking your rock stars what motivates them and then enabling them around those factors. Put the pieces in place. Help them to grow their careers. Show that you're invested in them from a long-term perspective.

Committing to career growth means that some of your best reps will transition to leadership. The question is, when that happens, is it going to cripple your sales organization, or will you have other budding, talented leaders waiting in the wings, ready to step up and take charge?

As a sales leader, I get the impulse to give the best leads to your rock stars. They have a demonstrated track record, and you know they can handle the work. It's an understandable impulse—one I followed in my days as a sales leader as well.

But while it's an understandable impulse, it's not a fair one—and it will set you up for failure in the long term. The more that you can level the playing field and plan the game where everyone benefits, the sooner you can escape the hero trap and get better contributions from your entire sales team. You don't need a hero when everyone is outperforming expectations.

Of course, as we'll see in the next chapter, this doesn't solve the problem completely. While ditching the hero culture mind-

---

23 Xactly, "The Sales Talent Crisis."

set will absolutely help keep your rock stars around longer (and help you level up new rock stars), there are a lot of other reasons why someone might leave their job.

After all, your top performers aren't valuable just to you. They're valuable to everyone. No matter the market, top performers will have no problem finding work elsewhere.

The question is, outside of creating a fair playing field, what else are you doing to keep them?

INTELLIGENT REVENUE TUNE-UPS

→ Does your company's sales performance resemble the bimodal distribution curve? How can you address this?

→ What are ways you can remove assumptions from planning and increase accuracy?

→ How does your company create benchmarks? Do they align with your actual trajectory?

CHAPTER 8

FORECAST WITH CONFIDENCE

BACK IN THE OLD DAYS WHEN I WAS THE HEAD OF SALES
at a software company, I took pride in my ability to master the
dark arts and call the ball with accuracy.

But here's the big secret: I wasn't that accurate. I usually
came within 15 percent of our final number—plus or minus.

By industry standards, that was pretty good. Not great, but
pretty good.

The real rock stars are able to call the ball within 10 percent.
The not-so-great ones? They're usually off by 30 to 40 percent.

Think about that kind of variance for a minute: 20 percent
(10 percent in either direction) if you're a rock star, 30 percent
if you're considered decent, and as much as 80 percent if you're
mediocre.

Even for the rock stars, that's huge variability. In that kind of
environment, how is your CFO supposed to make any decisions
with confidence?

Whether you're under your number or over it, that's bad for

business. If you tell your board your sales team will generate $10 million in the upcoming quarter, then a final number of $8 million won't sit well—and it sure won't help your poor CFO rest any easier.

But, believe it or not, overshooting your forecast is just as bad. If you predict a $10 million quarter and wind up doing $14 million, you still look like you don't know your business and are operating based on luck. The next quarter, whatever number you give, your CFO, your CEO, and the board simply won't believe you. In fact, they'll likely assume you underestimated on purpose to make the final numbers look better.

I'm sure some sales leaders do that, but most are trying to make an honest prediction. The problem, as we'll see in this chapter, is that sales leaders following the traditional model don't have much to go off of other than the faulty reporting of their reps and their own gut.

Now, you could have a great gut. But it's only going to help you if the information you're working with is lousy. And with all due respect to most revenue operations, it usually is.

And yet, from this lousy information, CEOs, CFOs, and boards routinely cross their fingers and hope that the forecast will be close enough that they aren't left high and dry. This is a herculean task, one that only 6 percent of sales leaders actually feel confident in doing. And yet, whatever number they come up with, that's what the organization builds around.

Suffice it to say, that's no way to build a quality revenue operation. You can have the best go-to-market strategy in the world. You can incentivize the exact behaviors that will generate quality sales for your organization. But to generate quality revenue, you have to be able to predict and hit your target with greater accuracy.

Fortunately, younger generations of sales leaders are waking up to that fact. Sure, they still take pride in calling the ball well, but they'd prefer some data and AI-driven insights to help make that call a little more accurately. It's another component to add to their repertoire, and they're happy to embrace it.

With the right tools and, more importantly, an Intelligent Revenue approach, you can forecast both quicker and more effectively. In this chapter, we're going to strip the voodoo and dark arts from your forecasting function and help you build a more elegant, data-focused approach.

Almost all sales interactions are now intermediated by technology. Reps utilize email, instant messaging, and record phone and video calls. Because of how our world has embraced these technological aspects, we can capture data with each and every interaction. We'd be utterly foolish not to. In turn, we almost have no choice—if we want to stay competitive—to apply this rich dataset to forecasting. Software can directly observe, aggregate, and analyze customer interactions and in turn the health of deals and their likelihood to close. Any sales leader who refuses to do this is leaving a massive opportunity on the table.

Organizations make big decisions based on their sales forecasts, often to disastrous results when they over- or undershoot their number. An Intelligent Revenue approach to forecasting uses feedback from several sources within a company to improve planning and performance.

We don't take forecasting lightly, and neither should you. The consequences for missing the mark move like a shock wave through your entire organization.

A HIGH-STAKES GUESSING GAME

In order to understand how an Intelligent Revenue approach can improve an organization's Prediction ability, first it's important to better understand the cascading problem most revenue operations find themselves in.

Imagine that your organization has two hundred sales reps, each of whom is working twenty to fifty opportunities at once. Within this group, each rep will report on the small handful of deals they think will close. This in itself is always in flux, and their reporting is usually based on a hunch—or at best, a poorly designed set of metrics.

From the moment the rep makes their prediction, they're essentially making a commitment to their sales manager, who in turn gets similar commitments from their other reps. If ten reps each predict roughly $100,000 in closed deals, then their overall commitment is $1 million. The manager then rolls up those commitments to $1.5 million and reports that number to their boss, who, after hearing reports from other managers, then hedges that number and takes it down to $900,000.

And so on. The higher the number goes up the chain, the more it gets either rolled up or hedged. By the time it gets up to the CEO and CFO, it's usually wildly off—the result of a compounding voodoo effect.

Depending on your team's overall attitude toward risk, that number could either be ultraconservative or ultra-aggressive. But either way, it doesn't have a reliable relationship to reality. It's based on ten separate hunches. No one knows the truth.

Time passes, some deals fall through, some get lost to competitors, and others close. Often, the deals the reps expected to close never materialize—and the deals they hadn't put much stock in are suddenly big winners. There's a constant state of flux in the numbers as deals come and go.

In such an environment, no one knows what's actually going on; they just hope and pray the head of sales has their arms around the situation and has called the ball in a way that sufficiently anticipates all the different variables. The company is going to take whatever numbers the head of sales comes up with and run with them.

With so much pressure to call the ball, it's no surprise that everyone around the head of sales is working their own predictive magic as well. They know the company's forecast depends heavily on one person's ability to call the ball accurately, and they all have various degrees of confidence in their head of sales to do just that. If, for instance, Head of Sales Johnny says the company is on track for $10 million for the quarter, his boss might slightly discount that number, because Johnny has historically always overestimated. The inverse could happen as well.

It's a giant cloud of squishy, emotional guessing on the part of the head of sales, because none of the numbers are reliable. It's also a lot of pressure; how well they can guess through all that intense uncertainty literally determines their tenure in the organization.

With that being said, why on earth would any organization choose to do things this way? Flying by the seat of your pants is no way to build quality revenue. Again, everything comes back to the data.

WHY ISN'T THERE BETTER DATA?

Now that we've explored the problem, let's turn our attention to the culprit: customer relationship management tools (CRMs). When you're using a tool that, to be frank, doesn't have very good predictive capabilities, you have no choice but to use a little bit of voodoo—or a lot of voodoo—in order to call the ball.

This isn't to say CRMs are worthless, of course. Everyone uses tools from Salesforce, Oracle, or Microsoft to manage their opportunities. It's just that these tools weren't built for forecasting—at least, not in a way that drives insights and leads to quality revenue.

Most CRMs operate on a moment-in-time paradigm. They can tell you what your pipeline looks like on a particular moment on a particular day, but they can't tell you what the pipeline looked like yesterday—or where it may be headed tomorrow.

As you can imagine, this leads to a lot of consternation. The sales team may head home on Friday with $10 million forecasted to close only to find on Monday that the number has shrunk to $9 million—and with only moment-in-time reporting, they'll have no idea what changed. Needless to say, when your tool isn't built to offer many insights, it's a forensic nightmare to figure out what happened, especially if you have a large sales team.

This is why, even with a CRM, sales leaders have so much difficulty calling the ball. How can you when your forecasts only offer a narrow picture of your pipeline?

Without a better tool, you can't.

WHAT DOES A GOOD FORECASTING TOOL DO?

Imagine you've got a crystal ball. That crystal ball can tell you with startling accuracy what the economy is going to look like twelve, eighteen, even twenty-four months into the future.

That kind of predictive ability isn't just good for letting you know whether your sales are on track right now. It's your chance to determine your future risk and put the work in now to correct it.

Go look at your numbers over the last five quarters. For each quarter, what was the sales call at the beginning, and what was the actual number at the end?

Were you ever close—even if only for a single quarter? If so, you're in rare company. For most organizations, those numbers are often very far apart.

I don't mind going to my bosses and saying I'm going to miss my number. But I do need to be prepared to answer the very next question that's going to come out of their mouths: "By how much?"

Naturally, this is the exact question I'm going to ask my CRO before I approach my bosses. Any good CRO should be able to not only give me a number but articulate it with some sense of accuracy.

Unfortunately, not many leaders are able to do that. According to Gartner, only 6 percent of CROs are confident they're going to make their call. To be clear, none of them will make the number they predict.

How does a CEO run a business on a number they can't rely on? How would they even know what to do next?

They don't. That's why you see all these knee-jerk reactions, with organizations cutting large swaths of their workforce in part because they'd rather be safe than sorry and in part because they can't trust the numbers they've been given to work with.

Proper forecasting could limit these knee-jerk reactions, not to mention allow leaders to feel much better about their numbers. This is a nonnegotiable piece of Intelligent Revenue. No more relying on gut instincts over cold, hard facts.

A good forecasting tool will roll up all sales data from each rep deal by deal—what they're committing, what they're forecasting, etc. Then the tool will take all that information and spit out a forecast.

Many tools, such as Salesforce, are already capable of doing exactly that. Aggregating sales data is a good first step. However, the best forecasting tools take things a step further, incorporating data and AI to create their projections. That's how information leads to insight.

Often, these AI-driven projections will be different from

what their human counterparts come up with. Using the same information, for instance, the head of sales might commit to $36 million in quarterly revenue.

The AI tool, however, knows how to dig a little bit deeper, looking at dozens of different inputs to come up with its number, such as these:

- Who's forecasting these deals?
- What's their track record?
- How long has a deal been forecasted?
- How quickly has the deal been moving through?
- How many calls and interactions have there been with customers?
- Using historical data of similar deals, what patterns can we see in buyer behavior?

These AI tools even have the ability to read buyer sentiments in phone calls or email interactions between the customer and sales rep, looking for phrases like "Hallelujah!," "This is cool," "We love it," or the killers: "It's really fricking expensive," or "I don't have budget to buy this."

Once the tool runs through these inputs, it spits out a revised forecast along with a deal-by-deal breakdown of which deals are likely to close and which ones are in danger.

The result is what every CRO craves but few are able to deliver: accuracy. And according to Intangent, companies with accurate forecasts are 10 percent more likely to grow revenue year-over-year.[24] By focusing on Intelligent Revenue, then, organizations are not only able to sustain revenue, but also to grow it.

---

24   Intangent, "6 Shocking Statistics about Sales Forecasting," accessed September 8, 2023, https://www.intangent.com/blog/6-shocking-statistics-about-sales-forecasting.

CALLING THE BALL WITH CONVICTION

To recap so far: the forecasting system essentially amounts to sales reps making their best guess on what deals will close, their bosses adding their own guesses based on feedback from several reps, their bosses adding their own best guess, and so on until it's time for the sales lead to call the ball and pray they were right.

You can see how small inaccuracies have a way of compounding as they move up the chain of command. It's like a game of telephone with millions of dollars—and potentially a company's livelihood—on the line.

Some sales leaders are good at this strange voodoo, but most aren't, which leads to a lot of consternation at the highest levels of the business about whether they're going to make their number. No one particularly likes this strange voodoo, but because everyone's relying on the same CRM options as everyone else, no one has much of a choice.

Now, let's see what this same dynamic, ever-changing prediction process looks like in the context of Intelligent Revenue.

The differences start at the rep level. Whereas previously, a rep would make their best guess about which three or so deals might close soon out of the thirty they're working, now they have the added insights of AI and machine learning to support these guesses.

This intelligent forecasting system uses pattern recognition based on historical data—the rep's, the organization's, and other organizations' as well. If a deal looks likely to close, an integrated tool will flag it, explain why, and offer suggestions on what to do next. If a deal looks to be in danger, again it will flag it, highlight factors the rep may not be aware of, and offer insights on what steps other reps took to rescue similar deals in the past. As a result, the reps can adjust their behavior and tilt the odds in their favor.

Because the system is running this exact same program for every rep, these insights are multiplied across the sales organization. The system will then look at all the in-progress deals in aggregate, rolling all the way up to senior management, and provide a fact- and data-based opinion on the numbers.

Now, because Intelligent Revenue tools don't operate on a moment-in-time paradigm, sales leaders can also examine the historical trajectory of their pipeline. Want to see what the forecast was two weeks ago compared to today? Just dial it back to view a snapshot and review all the deals to see which went up, down, or sideways.

Through an IR tool, not only do sales leaders have better visibility into what changed from day to day, but they also have better insight into why these changes happened. Are several big deals in danger of going off the rails, or have they simply pushed to next quarter? Do certain reps keep losing deals at similar points in the pipeline? Whatever the case, the sales leader will have a much easier time getting to the core of the issue and addressing the root concern, whether through changing tactics, coaching a rep, and so on.

To be clear, an Intelligent Revenue approach doesn't replace a CRM like Salesforce. Those are still useful tools for what they're designed to do. Rather, a good planning tool sits on top of this CRM, running that platform's data through its own program in order to generate additional real-time insights.

Is this system designed to call the ball and replace the head of sales? Not at all. Again, some heads of sales are quite good at forecasting, despite having to rely so much on their gut. Rather than replace the head of sales, Intelligent Revenue augments the head of sales's expertise, helping them to craft a much more accurate forecast within a much narrower band of outcomes.

In other words, the head of sales already has their gut. Now they have another tool—one built around the data from thousands of other heads of sales who have also had to call the ball in similar situations. This is a valuable competitive advantage. Whereas CFOs, heads of sales, and corporate planners all have basic models based on their own intuition and experience, they're still limited to their own experiences and body of knowledge. An Intelligent Revenue approach leverages not just one person's experience, but every user's experience.

This type of forecasting tool, in other words, isn't the final word. It's just one assessment. At Xactly, we take the feedback from our IR tools; we take the forecast from our sales leaders; and then we settle on our final target.

The result? Greater accuracy, more predictability, and greater quality of revenue. Instead of trying to make do within a 30 percent forecasting variance, you can move forward confidently with a 5 percent variance. Some Xactly clients even report forecasting accuracy at nearly 100 percent.

Beyond the numbers, however, is the change in the workplace that Intelligent Revenue can help bring about: greater transparency, improved behaviors, and healthier relationships. When you forecast near 100 percent accuracy, you're treated differently within a company. If the board knows 94 percent of forecasts are inaccurate, the conversation isn't going to go well. If you flip that percentage to 90 percent accurate using augmented intelligence, you foster more trust—and in turn, you get more done.

Lastly, there's the time savings. A good planning tool allows sales leaders to work both faster and more accurately, freeing them up to spend more of their time on other efforts that could help grow revenue.

SEPARATING THE GOLD FROM THE NOISE

Imagine you've been selling to an account and anticipate a deal will close in four weeks. You have another call with the buyer, and you think it went well. Then the conversational intelligence engine raises a flag: the buyer mentioned your competitor three times.

You missed these mentions. You didn't even note them in your call logs. You had your eyes on the prize, and because of that, you weren't thinking as objectively as you could be. Your augmented intelligence tool, however, wasn't fooled. Because of this input, it drops your probability of closing from 90 percent to 75 percent.

That's got your attention. After all, your commission just went from a sure thing to a less-than-sure thing.

Fortunately, now that you have more insight into buyer sentiment, you also have a perfect opportunity to be proactive and get the deal back on track.

In the old model, this never would have happened. Had you lost the deal, you would have had no idea how it went south—and few clues in the call notes stored in your CRM.

Augmented intelligence gives you more insights, allowing you to refine your forecast and drive behavioral change at scale. In this example, based on your experience with this customer, your sales leads could then train the entire sales team to listen more closely for competitor mentions. Not only do you know exactly what happened and why in terms of your own deal, but you can also use that knowledge to help everyone do better moving forward.

IMPROVE COACHING

So how can more accurate forecasting lead to such a big revenue bump? In short, because the clearer you can see into the future, the more you can intervene to improve your range of possible outcomes.

Here's an example. Say your data tells you that one of your

sales reps isn't making their calls at the rate you recommend. Okay, might not be a big deal now; they're still well on track to hit their goals for the quarter. But here's the thing: those missed calls are a lagging indicator of future risk. Everything might be fine now, but six months from now when there aren't enough deals in your pipeline, you'll be left scratching your head trying to figure out why.

Through a combination of data-driven insights and effective coaching, you can mitigate risks like this. Using their intelligent forecasting system, a rep could zoom in on any given deal and find a variety of insights waiting for them. For instance, say the rep is working on a deal that has a 60 percent probability of closing. With one click, the program would list out the reasons the deal is likely to close and then list out the reasons it's unlikely to close.

What might this look like? Many of the reasons a deal succeeds or fails involve price. Price sensitivity varies among buyers and industries, and it also matters how your product is positioned with regard to competitors.

A sales rep's relationship with the customer makes a difference. Like it or not, charisma can be just as big a part of selling as product knowledge in some instances. Having that bond with the customer and picking up on key phrases during sales calls—like in the earlier example—change the likelihood of a deal closing.

Finally, where your company is positioned in the industry matters. There's often an established market leader, an alpha dog that has it a little bit easier than competitors. Is that your company? How do you know for sure? Intelligent revenue-focused tools can take this into account when forecasting a deal's chances of success.

Sometimes, all these tools do is surface the obvious. For

instance, if the rep had put in a close date that's already come and gone, then the software will flag that as a negative factor and offer the rep suggestions for getting the deal back into the green—and therefore make it much more likely to close. Through these coaching features, reps will learn how to forecast much more accurately.

TYING FORECASTING TO COMP

Many sales leaders think forecasting is all about calling the number. That's a piece of it, but when you're targeting a rule of 40 or rule of 50 in terms of revenue (yearly revenue growth plus EBITDA growth), that can't be all you look at. After all, you could be hitting all your sales numbers, but if your comp expenses are also high, then that number might not end up being as impressive as you'd hoped. Another way to grow revenue, then, is not just to chase that top-line number, but to work with the CFO to create a commission forecast as well.

If you have a system that's fully integrated between the different functions of your revenue operation, then you can tie your forecasting abilities to the comp payout your rep will receive. Say, for instance, that you have a hundred deals you know are going to close soon. You know which reps are closing those deals, and you know where they are in their year.

If your system can't tell you where your reps are on their comp plans and what deals you have in the pipeline, then as the CFO, you're far more likely to play conservative. You'll over-accrue because you aren't sure how much you need to pay out all outstanding commissions.

Under-accruing is bad—you always need to be able to pay out your sales reps—but over-accruing is just as bad. Missing your number is still missing your number. It's better to be accurate.

Now that you understand a little of what automated intelligence can do in terms of forecasting, let's build on that conversation and discuss some more advanced capabilities—in this case, a capability that one of our own customers led us to.

A few years ago, we noticed that one of our biggest customers—we'll call them VIP Power—was doing something odd. They kept copying their data into a non-payroll sandbox environment and running their numbers over and over again. Unknown to VIP Power, this was putting a tremendous load on our databases. So we reached out to them to learn what was going on.

Their answers surprised us. Like many large companies, VIP Power's number-two item on the balance sheet behind payroll was their variable commission expense. Depending on the bonus structures in place, as well as which salesperson was getting paid out, this expense could vary quite a bit.

This variance made the people at VIP Power uneasy. As a public company, their ability to close their books and forecast their earnings per share could sway the results on an earnings-per-share basis by one or two points in either direction—all based on whether they were going to be paying out a large percentage of commissions.

VIP Power wanted better insights into what sort of variances they could expect. Like many companies, their salespeople closed quite a few deals during the last week of every quarter. They wanted to know what the different scenarios looked like in terms of how many deals might close and who was expected to close them. So they began using our sandbox to simulate different orders and model different scenarios in order to forecast what their commission expense was going to be.

This thinking made a lot of sense. After all, a company hitting its forecast tells only part of the story. How did it hit its numbers? Did half the sales team dramatically overachieve the sales plan, hitting accelerator after accelerator to land themselves an especially hefty payout? Or did the other half of the sales team dramatically underachieve, riding on the coattails of the overachievers and hoping no one would notice?

Think about what a scenario like that would do to your own variable compensation expenses. Sure, in either scenario, you hit your overall target. But it's going to cost you a lot more to do it in the former scenario than in the latter. Last time I checked with my finance team, spending more than you thought you were going to spend—for the same amount of projected revenue—isn't a good way to generate quality revenue.

CFOs like predictability. Their job is to make sure every part of the company has the financial resources they need, and to do that, they need to be confident that the forecast is accurate, and so is the variable compensation plan.

Unfortunately, just like with forecasting in general, CFOs haven't had much insight into the latter. Sure, you could make a prediction, but otherwise you'd have to wait and see which deals closed, who closed them, what accelerators they were on, and what their payout was. And you'd have to do everything manually. Finally, after all that, you could run the numbers, cross your fingers, and hope you weren't too far over or under in either direction.

VIP Power thought this process sounded tedious. Then they realized they could get a more accurate result simply by using an existing tool to game out different compensation scenarios. That way, their finance team wasn't left holding the purse at the end of the quarter.

As soon as we saw what they were doing, we immediately jumped in to help. Soon, we had built out a new tool: Commission Expense Forecasting.

CASE STUDY: APPTIO

In just a month's time, Apptio was on the path to dramatically improving its financial accuracy and sales performance. Founded in 2007, the 1,300-person company Apptio serves its customers with a unique suite of financial tools to help its clients make better investment decisions.

But while their product was good, their revenue operation was a three-ring circus. At the circus, viewers may thrill to watch performers juggling or spinning plates while acrobats pull off death-defying stunts overhead. At a tech company, however, these theatrics are not only nerve-racking but dangerous.

And yet, that's precisely what they were experiencing as sales teams found themselves juggling multiple data reporting systems, each of which captured data and refreshed their projections differently. The only way for sales and finance leaders to get a clear sense of the current forecast was to compare and contrast the outputs from all these competing tools. Such work is not only tedious and error prone, but it's also time consuming. It's no wonder, then, that Apptio's sales organization was experiencing such a high churn rate.

With Xactly's forecasting tool, Apptio was able to create a single, reliable view of all their data. This allowed their leadership team and their sales representatives to collaborate from the same starting point. Leadership had a "single pane of glass" to look at all sales activity, while rep-level employees were able to develop helpful templates and fashion helpful reports through a simple, plug-and-play interface.

This change provided Apptio with a single, reliable tool with which to house and analyze all their data. Of course, Apptio's adoption of this new tool was about more than just the metrics. It was about streamlining and collating activities. By limiting the time people spend juggling information, Apptio could provide centralized data for senior leadership in real time.

With Commission Expense Forecasting, finance now has a tool that allows them to see and predict variable compensation payouts as they go. As a result, they can accurately predict what the commission expense will be as a line item on the balance sheet. With the ability to model different scenarios, finance teams gain a greater understanding of what their over-all expenses are going to be for the month, quarter, or year. Not only does this give them greater insight into their business, but it also works to keep shareholders happy—which, I'm told, is always a good thing.

If you're spending $2 billion in variable commission pay-ments alone each year, then this kind of forecasting isn't only a good idea; it's essential. After all, a forecast swing of even a couple of points would mean millions of dollars in your quar-terly or annual report. And remember: an automated tool can not only help with your commission expense forecasting, but can also help with making sure you're getting the most out of those $2 billion in variable commissions by driving the behaviors that will ultimately boost your bottom line.

ANOTHER TOOL IN YOUR BELT

In a 2022 blog post, former Minor League Baseball player—and current Xactly Sales Director—Taylor Wilding compared modern selling to *Moneyball*. In case you're not familiar with the term, Moneyball is a practice popularized in baseball by former Oakland Athletics General Manager Billy Beane that applied advanced statistical analysis to identify high-value players that the team could then recruit, sign, or trade for in order to get the greatest value for the lowest overall cost.

Of course, players still have to pass the eye test. There are still hours and hours of tape to watch, workouts to oversee, and conversations to be had with the players themselves. Money-ball doesn't replace the importance of scouting and coaching. It just augments their ability to do a good job. At the end of the day, the best coaches use all the data and tools at their disposal, not just their gut. As a result, they make better decisions more consistently for the team they represent.[25]

This is the difference between successful sales leaders and mediocre ones. The mediocre leaders stick to the same bag of tricks they've always known, while the successful leaders are always looking for a new advantage, some new insight to help direct and validate their own instincts.

It's a flawed way of thinking to believe you're so amazing that you don't need any help. No matter how intelligent and experienced you are, you don't have the computational capacity to look at millions of data points in real time. You don't have the time in your schedule to listen to every single sales call your team makes. But if you have access to a tool that can do these things both better and more quickly than you ever could, then why would you leave that tool on the table?

There's no need to feel threatened by data-driven forecasting. No one is trying to replace you and the value you bring. Instead, think of this tool as just another arrow in your quiver—along with your relationships with your sales reps, your knowledge of their skills, your awareness of subtle buying signs, and, of course, your instincts.

Don't let pride be the reason you don't make full use of your arsenal. Don't let pride be the reason your organization settles for a 20 percent forecasting variance when you could narrow the results dramatically in your favor. The consequences of inaccuracy—and inaction—are massive in terms of decision-making, business performance, and, ultimately, your trajectory as a sales leader.

So which path will you choose?

To me, it's a no-brainer.

------

25 Taylor Wilding, "Shifting Your Revenue Performance Starts with a World Series Mindset," Xactly, January 13, 2022.

INTELLIGENT REVENUE TUNE-UPS

→ Do you have a data problem? How does this make it more difficult for your head of sales to call the ball?

→ How could more accurate forecasting help your company transition to a quality revenue operation?

→ Are variable compensation expenses a source of worry at your company? What's one way automated intelligence could mitigate this?

→ What insights is your company missing when it comes to planning for the future?

CHAPTER 9

STOP THE ATTRITION

ONE DAY, OUR CTO LOOKED AT OUR DATA AND TOLD ME that one of our tools was predicting that one of our top reps in Europe was about to quit.

"No way," I said. "The algorithm must be broken. That guy's already at 110 percent of his quota."

Well, guess what? He quit that very weekend. Algorithm one, Cabrera zero.

No AI or machine learning tool will be accurate 100 percent of the time. But they can give you a good sense of the likelihood of certain outcomes, which can help organizations better plan for the future. If the data shows that one of your top performers is headed out the door, then you can either work to intervene or find their replacement.

In the case of attrition and turnover, think about the impact a little advance knowledge can have in terms of hiring and ramp-up time. If you know six months out how many people you expect to lose, you can have your replacements already trained and ready to go when the dominoes start to fall—all without sacrificing any momentum. And if your attrition ends up trending higher than the initial projection, you'll get a jump on that insight too.

In the competitive post-pandemic market, planning for attrition is more important than ever. Unfortunately, most revenue operations still don't take the issue seriously enough. They set their plan and then they lock it away. The targets are never updated, even if the reality has dramatically changed just a few weeks or months later.

Think of the cost to your organization if your attrition rate is double your projection. Sure, there's the revenue lost, especially if you've lost a top performer. But there's also the additional ramp-up time you didn't plan for—not to mention the additional three months it might take you to find the right replacement.

What you don't plan for—or what you don't adapt to—can kill you. If you're working off a fixed plan, this can have a serious impact on your organization, putting you so far behind on the year that you have no realistic strategy for catching up. With a system that can adjust the plan in the face of unexpected change, however, you have a chance to get out there, find your next generation of sales reps, and ramp them up within the company.

The concept of preparing for the unexpected has never been more important. When it comes to holding onto the people that keep your company running, these are unprecedented times.

Call it the Great Resignation, call it Quiet Quitting, call it whatever the popular term of the day is (and there's *always* a new trendy term), but sales organizations face a real challenge attracting and retaining top talent. In this chapter, readers will learn to adopt an Intelligent Revenue approach to building a shared culture of top performers.

Remember, Intelligent Revenue boils down to technology, tactics, and alignment. Your organization's alignment—from the very top down to the newest hire—is critical in the shift from unsustainable growth to quality revenue that lasts. How you implement that positive culture is everything.

The world is changing. People at all levels of the workforce are reporting unprecedented burnout. Meanwhile, that workforce is becoming increasingly remote. New tactics are required to engage, incentivize, and support that workforce, and it's up to your leadership to drive that change.

WE LIVE IN EXASPERATING TIMES

The men and women running your sales organizations are exasperated right now.

Attrition represents one of the great existential threats to the modern sales organization.

In 2022, Xactly surveyed over five hundred sales leaders at over four hundred companies. From that survey, we learned that, between 2018 and 2020, over 150,000 people had attrited from these companies. And the attrition rates were getting worse. Between 2018 and 2019, the average attrition rate at these companies was 15 to 20 percent. In 2020, that number had grown to 25 to 40 percent.

As for the employees who were sticking around? Not much reason for optimism there either. Our study found that, of the over five hundred sales leaders that we surveyed, 88 percent were willing to leave, and 48 percent were *likely* to leave.

Now ask yourself, what happens to your organization when so much of your top talent is either headed out the door or already has one foot out the door? Any way you slice it, the answer isn't good.

So why are so many of your sales leaders willing to leave?

Simply put, it's not fun to be in sales right now. It's not fun to be in a sales organization right now, and it's not fun to be *leaving* a sales organization right now.

Why is that? While sales, just like any other facet of an economy, can be cyclical, some of the factors making sales rough in the present aren't going to go away. It's a buyer's world, and increased competition only gives more leverage to the buyer. In particular, the explosion of SaaS companies and the market saturation that comes with that only adds to the stress of a sales rep's job.

Sales has always been a grind, but uncertainty and increased turnover have given that a new meaning.

This may seem like a basic point, but it's essential to support your go-to-market team with the right mindset. If all you're doing is talking trash about the performance of your sales team, then you're going to be in a world of hurt. Why? Because you're missing the point. While it's never okay to excuse underperformance, if you don't understand the external factors that are leading to your numbers, then you won't be able to effectively address the problem.

THE ENDLESS ATTRITION CYCLE

When it comes to salespeople, it's a buyer's market. This was true when my first book came out back in 2014, and it's still true today. I wish it weren't so, but there just aren't enough good salespeople. And with everyone eager to secure the talents of the top salespeople that are out there, salespeople have a lot more power than they used to.

Here's the basic progression. Rock star sales rep Joan works for Company X. One day, Company Y lures Joan away with a better base salary and compensation plan. This is a big get for Company Y...until Company Z comes along a couple of months

later and lures Joan to *their* sales team with an even more enticing package.

No one wins in this environment, not even Company Z, who
could easily lose Joan to someone else. Sure, you could argue that
Joan wins in this situation, and in some ways she does, but it's
not easy switching organizations every few months, learning new
systems, new product mixes, and new organizational cultures.

Attrition has always been a reality in any sales operation. But
it's become a much bigger problem in recent years. Despite this,
we believe that it's dangerous—and costly—to treat this kind of
attrition as inevitable.

I probably don't need to tell you how much time it takes to
find new qualified salespeople, train them, and then to wait
patiently until they ramp up into their first sale. This process
for just a single person can take the better part of a year. If
you're constantly caught in this cycle, not only are you racing
to replace your biggest producers, but you're expending considerable resources just trying to get your new producers up to
speed. The result? A revenue operation that's never quite firing
on all cylinders.

That doesn't mean you should panic over every employee—
your B and C players included—you lose to better opportunities.
Great Resignation or not, some turnover is bound to happen,
and it doesn't necessarily have to keep you behind the eight
ball. Congratulate them on their success and wish them luck.
Meanwhile, you're using intelligent systems to predict this turnover, hire, and train the next group, some of which will produce
great results.

Your top players, however, are much harder to replace. You
should be doing everything in your power to hold onto them.
Losing these pieces is not only costly, but is the most surefire
way to keep your revenue operation lagging behind its goals.

It doesn't have to be this way. Contrary to popular belief, salespeople aren't purely coin operated. Yes, you need to offer a competitive plan. But research shows that salespeople don't stay with or leave companies based on pay alone. In fact, a lot of it comes down to trust. Unfortunately, as you'll see, most revenue operations have a long way to go to earn that trust.

PEOPLE QUIT BAD CULTURES

Looking back, the Great Resignation was pretty short lived. The people who were on the front end were just chasing the money; many people found they could get $50,000 more to do the same job somewhere else, and they leaped at the opportunity.

On the one hand, who could blame them? Go get paid and take care of your family. On the other hand, as a business leader, this was a scary time. How were we supposed to compete with that? The difference was so stark, we couldn't even make a counteroffer.

Then, just as quickly as it began, the Great Resignation was over.

Part of the reason was due to a shift in the economy. After the surprising growth period during the height of the COVID-19 pandemic, inflation reared its ugly head in a big way, and suddenly the business world was staring down the prospect of recession. Instead of scrambling to hire as many warm bodies as they could, businesses were laying off parts of their workforce.

The other part was something a little more intangible, something I like to refer to as "The Great Regret." Employees who had left their companies thinking the grass was greener somewhere else (and with a higher salary) suddenly realized they were better off where they were. And so, these "boomerang" employees found a new regard for their former workplace and the courage to ask for their old jobs back.

This happened at Xactly, too, and I was happy to let these talented team members come back. Some leaders thought I was crazy to do so, but think about it: Why wouldn't you want to welcome back a team member who now had a much deeper appreciation for the company and their job?

Here's the thing: good employees that value your company's culture are hard to come by. There's a common misconception that sales professionals are driven only by compensation. But compensation alone is no longer enough to retain top talent in a tight labor market. You have to offer something more.

Again, the data bears this out. An Xactly survey found that roughly 66 percent of sales leaders would leave their current job for an equivalent role at a more purposeful or values-aligned company. A Gartner survey of workers found similar results, with 56 percent indicating a greater interest in contributing to society, and 52 percent wondering whether their day job allowed them to do that.

People want purpose. The best salespeople are probably going to have success anywhere they go. In order to lure the top dogs—the A-team players—what can you offer that other companies can't, or don't? Showing you care about your employees, and that they can grow and prosper in your company, is a big step in the right direction.

None of this is to say compensation isn't important. It is. But think of big compensation like a shiny lure. It may entice and hook the fish, but it doesn't keep the fish around in the long term. Over time, a company's work environment and culture become much more important. And, like we've stressed, you need to retain a significant portion of your sales team so you're not constantly rehiring and retraining—especially the top performers.

Intelligent Revenue companies stay ahead of the attrition that keeps a revenue engine lagging behind peak performance by addressing employee concerns. So if compensation isn't the be-all, end-all, why do employees leave? As our survey found, chalk up the attrition to poor work–life balance, lack of career opportunities, bad company culture, poor management, and stress or burnout. Ignoring these problems doesn't fix them, nor can they be completely eliminated. Sales is stressful. Even so, we can get ahead of our biggest obstacles. Poor management and bad culture? We can definitely improve in these areas if needed.

We talked earlier about beginning with the end in mind. You should absolutely do this with your employees. Salespeople are expensive to find, hire, and train. When you hire a new rep, where do you see their career three, four, or five years down the road? What is your goal for that employee? Better yet, how will the initial—costly—investment you made in them translate into a sizable return for your company?

You'll never know if you can't keep them around. Or keep them productive.

SUPPORT YOUR TEAMS ON THEIR TERMS

I hate the term "quiet quitting." I don't think it's right to apply these cutesie terms to what are ultimately real problems that affect real people. Acting in a way that negatively impacts productivity, performance, and morale doesn't only hurt the employee who is "quiet quitting," but everyone else within the organization as well. As business leaders, we shouldn't make light of that. But it's the term the internet has chosen to discuss this phenomenon, so we might as well work with it.

Admittedly, I was unsure of exactly what this term meant when I first heard it. Initially, I thought it meant that your employees had essentially quit their jobs, but they just hadn't told you yet. As the conversation evolved, I came to understand that it wasn't that quiet quitters had stopped working entirely, but rather that they were doing only the bare minimum to skate by.

Most conversations I heard about quiet quitting were always framed in the negative. How dare these people who just assume that skating by is okay?

I don't see it that way.

What if quiet quitting is just people standing up for their families, their health, and their lives? Is it a bad thing that more and more people don't think it's okay to subject themselves to eighty-hour workweeks that result in little-to-no material benefit to them?

COVID-19 changed the way that companies operate. There's never going to be a full return to the pre-2020 status quo. Most employees don't need to be in the office five days a week from eight to five o'clock. As long as they're putting in the work and getting results, who cares when or where the work is done?

Most of the CEOs I speak with are struggling with this new paradigm. Some have interpreted this shift to the extreme and eliminated all offices. Others have fought against the change and insisted that their employees return to the office full time. I tend to fall somewhere in the middle. I don't see a future where Xactly eliminates all its offices entirely, but I also don't see a reason to force people back into our offices simply to satisfy some arbitrary status quo.

But there's no need to guess here either. When we at Xactly were considering how best to approach this question, we did what we do best: gather data. Specifically, we sent out a survey to our employees asking what they preferred in terms of how they wanted to do their work.

The findings were telling. On the one hand, a full 60 percent of Xactly employees indicated that they had no interest in coming back to the office. Full stop. The other third of our employee base had very different opinions. They missed the camaraderie, they missed the interaction, and they wanted back into the office. For our company, at least, there was no middle ground: employees either wanted to keep working from home, or they wanted back in.

This got me thinking: Why had I been so concerned with getting everybody to return to in-person work? The only reason I could think of was that the company was paying all this rent for all these fancy offices, and I wanted to get my money's worth. That's stupid, old-fashioned thinking.

When considering the work-from-home/work-from-the-office debate, here's the best way to get your money's worth: support your employees in how they learn, how they think, and how they execute.

I do still think in-person work in the office is valuable, especially if you're in leadership. At our Los Gatos, California, office, for instance, we don't mandate that our team members come in. But many on our leadership team make it a point to be there in person every Tuesday and Thursday—even if it means sitting in traffic for an hour—and we regularly extend that invitation to others. Increasingly, more and more team members are accepting that invitation and showing up to the office. They miss the camaraderie.

I also believe that, with certain jobs in particular, in-person work supports a kind of deep, nuanced learning that many remote workers are missing out on. Call me biased, but I especially see this in sales. In my early days, when I was a telesales rep, I learned so much just by being in the office and listening over the wall to what our other reps were doing. I accept that in the modern workplace, I can't compel people to the office so that they can learn better by osmosis, but I do encourage aspiring sales leaders early in their careers not to discount the value of in-person interactions. This isn't to say that I think they should be in the office every day, just that it could be useful to find a remote/in-office balance that works for them.

However, this entire conversation relies on how your employees treat remote work. We can't ever assume any outcome is a given, especially when business leaders aren't present to actively supervise. In other words, don't take this new dynamic for granted.

When I first got my driver's license, I remember the person at the DMV saying, "This isn't a right. This is a privilege." That's still how I feel about remote work. I acknowledge the reality that we live in, and I know that remote work to some degree is both inevitable and—in some employees' minds, at least—nonnegotiable. But it's still a privilege, and that means the onus is on your team members to be accountable, to be productive, and to get their work done.

The rise of remote work means business leaders need to be more vigilant than ever. Quiet quitting in all its forms represents an existential threat to many of today's companies. This becomes easier when employees aren't face-to-face with their coworkers and sales leaders. Over time, they may become more comfortable making less calls, missing their numbers, and taking less initiative because no one is there to actively manage them.

Some nonperformers may even bank on the hope that a lack of face time will allow them to ride out the situation for six months, a year, or more before you finally fire them. As a business leader, you can't let this happen. Remote work isn't going anywhere. We can't let it become an excuse to fall short of goals. Accountability still matters.

YOU CAN'T WALK THE FLOOR ANYMORE

When I was a sales leader, I used to walk the floor with a clipboard (talk about old school), going cube to cube to check in with my sales reps. How were they doing? What was going well, and what wasn't? How were their deals progressing?

Not only was face time between supervisor and reps important, but making these rounds every day was convenient. We didn't have to schedule a time to meet or worry about time zones. Communication was instant.

These informal, person-to-person conversations were incredibly useful to me. They allowed me to get a gritty feel for the business. So when my boss would come to me and ask how things were going and what the plan was, I had such a strong feel for the business that I could answer from my gut—and my gut was usually right.

Much of that environment has gone away.

In a remote workforce, sales leaders can't walk the floor like they used to. As a result, that gritty feeling just isn't there—or at least, it's not nearly as reliable. Many leaders miss the old ways—and some have even gone so far as to question whether a modern sales operation can thrive in a remote work environment. How can anyone get a feel for how sales are going when the sales force is scattered across the country?

I get the complaint to a degree. After all, sales is a career where reps feed off of one another's energy. It's hard to replicate that sense of camaraderie and competition when reps don't share the same physical space.

But that doesn't mean it's impossible. Instead of pining for a bygone day that will likely never come back, I believe it's more valuable to adapt and grow. How can you carry the best elements of an in-person workforce into the new remote-first reality? I don't pretend to have all the answers, but here are a few things we're mindful of at Xactly.

First, keep celebrating the team's wins. Sales reps *love* to celebrate their wins. Sure, you may not be able to ring a gong in a remote environment, but there are absolutely ways you can still celebrate virtually. For instance, we make announcements on Slack and in email, we still celebrate in-person together at the end of the quarter, and we still host a President's Club. Use positive reinforcement to boost morale and steer behaviors in the right direction, just like you would in the office.

Second, if possible, schedule quarterly meetups to maintain motivation and culture and to reinforce bonds. Any in-person contact is probably beneficial. Your team may be predominantly virtual, but you can still use the few times you *are* together to strengthen bonds and get a feel for things.

CREATE A HEALTHY PIPELINE

According to our survey, one of the other reasons that top performers leave is that they don't believe the sales pipeline is there for them to make any money. (Yes, money isn't everything, but it is still a motivator.)

The solution to this is simple: keep a healthy pipeline, one that isn't overinflated or full of stalled-out deals. Help them to see the opportunity there, and they'll be far less likely to seek greener pastures somewhere else.

In order to do this, not only do you need an Intelligent Revenue approach that tracks sales data and territories in real time, but you need to convince your reps that they can rely on this system. By now, you should have been fostering that kind of trust with your team. If your top performers have concerns and you show them evidence of solid potential, odds are they'll believe you.

Be open and honest with your employees and share good data. It also goes a long way if you, as a company, care about what they care about.

CASE STUDY: METACOMPLIANCE

MetaCompliance is a leading cybersecurity and compliance specialist dedicated to helping organizations keep their staff safe online, secure their digital assets, and protect their corporate reputation. Its award-winning, cloud-based platform provides a one-stop-shop management solution to engage users, provide defense against cyber threats, and deliver regulator reporting.

In recent years, MetaCompliance has experienced tremendous growth—quickly expanding its sales team by 400 percent. To accommodate that growth, MetaCompliance partnered with Xactly to:

- Drive greater revenue predictability
- Eliminate intuition bias within the forecasting process and make data-driven decisions
- Achieve sales adoption of the product to boost clean data entry and improve forecasting data hygiene
- Enhance visibility to provide a more precise view of the pipeline

The result: certainty. Prior to working with Xactly, the MetaCompliance team saw forecasting as a guessing game. Now, they can call their number with confidence—enabling the company to not only grow quickly, but to grow right.

DO GOOD

In the last chapter, we mentioned a 2021 survey that we commissioned, which found that money was fifth on the average employee's priority list in terms of what would keep them at their current job. Ahead of money, coming in at number four, was the desire to see that their company was doing good in the world, regardless of industry.

This is an idea that Marc Benioff, co-founder of Salesforce, has championed through his "Pledge 1 Percent" movement. The idea here is simple: no matter your industry or your company size, commit to spending at least 1 percent of your revenue and resources to improve local communities.

At Xactly, we first joined this pledge by putting 1 percent of our founding shares into our 501(c)(3) foundation, XactlyOne, which organizes volunteer efforts and coordinates resources to assist communities in need. For example, in 2022, the Xactly-One Foundation worked to coordinate resources for hurricane relief in Puerto Rico. We've also worked with Habitat for Humanity and helped with local community art projects.

Doing good can't just be something your company waves its hand at by posting a page on your website filled with empty words and stock photos. It has to be embedded in the core of who you are and what you do. But don't worry: if you're reading this right now and you're worried that doing good *isn't* currently embedded in your company's DNA, that doesn't mean this is the end of the road for you. Companies can change. It's never too late to turn your focus to doing good.

Yes, it takes time, it's costly, and it is hard work. But you know what else takes time, is costly, and requires hard work? Turning people over. Make the effort to turn your company into a force for good, and you won't have to make nearly as much effort to retain, hire, and train your employees.

Just remember that you have to mean it. I've seen a lot of companies throw a lot of money at trying to create the appearance of wanting to do good. But you can tell it doesn't mean anything to the people at the top. Catchy slogans and splashy campaigns might fool a few people into sticking around, but more likely than not, people will see right through the effort.

YOUR TEAM MAKES ALL THE DIFFERENCE

We're not in a one-to-many world anymore. We're in a one-to-one world. Systems that are available today can allow you to customize your employees' experience in a way that you couldn't do back in the Stone Age of spreadsheets and good intentions—a Stone Age that, sadly, 70 percent of companies still find themselves in.

Your people are vitally important to your business. Not just as an expense, but because they make your revenue engine run. Without proper alignment, there is no quality revenue operation. Why? Because when you're constantly fighting attrition rather than building a culture focused on Intelligent Revenue, then you're never doing any work to move your sales operation forward.

Employees who care about the way your company does things will stick around and help an Intelligent Revenue operation see better results. They won't be worried about the sales pipeline or leaders overlooking their needs. Convince your top performers that your way is the best way, and you'll be a step closer to a quality revenue operation.

But to build your culture, you need to keep your thumb on the pulse of your company—and the bigger picture.

I said in Chapter 4, and I'll say it here: if you don't look at what's going on in the world right now, right in front of you, then you're hurting the value of your company. But here's the good news: you don't need to sit in a dark room with a flashlight and try to find your way through this. The data and best practices on how to stop the attrition and support and retain your team members is already out there. All you have to do is learn.

INTELLIGENT REVENUE TUNE-UPS

→ Is your company a positive work environment? How can you impact your employees' experience in a significant way?

→ Do you think your company's current approach to the remote/in-office work question is conducive to reaching your Intelligent Revenue goals?

→ How do you know if "quiet quitting" is a problem in your organization?

→ Do you know how your top performers feel about your company? How worried are they about your sales pipeline?

CHAPTER 10

THE FUTURE OF INTELLIGENT REVENUE

I'M A BIG FAN OF F1 RACING. ONE THING I LOVE ABOUT THE sport is how attentive the team is to every little detail. The teams responsible for building and maintaining those high-performance vehicles know that even a slight adjustment to the spoiler could mean the difference between winning and losing, so they're willing to put in the effort to give themselves the best chance.

Unfortunately, the business unicorns haven't figured this out yet. Businesses focused solely on plowing money into their company to grow at all costs often hope that if they just keep raising more capital, they can paper over all their warts in the process.

Rarely ever is that the case. In fact, often the opposite happens: the warts grow, the business loses viability, and eventually it goes under.

On the other end of the spectrum, businesses following an

Intelligent Revenue approach think a lot like an F1 team. They know that building a precision, high-functioning revenue operation requires a series of constant adjustments. Even a little tweak can make a tremendous difference to their bottom line, and so they're looking for every advantage they can get.

That's why, when they look at rising technologies like generative AI, they neither dismiss it as a fad nor fanatically jump on the bandwagon. Instead, they're pragmatic. How can they turn these tools to their advantage? How can these tools help their business do more with less, to squeeze every little bit of value out of their operation that they can?

When it comes to artificial intelligence, much of the story has yet to be written. Certainly, as I write this in mid-2023, AI is having a big moment—leading many to suspect its value is overhyped. In the short term, those skeptics are probably right. While everyone is scrambling to find novel ways to use AI for their business, the reality at present is their value is fairly limited.

In the long term, however, I believe AI is actually *under-hyped*. Decades from now, we're all going to look back at this moment and say, "This is when everything changed."

Consider Xactly's own story to understand why. In Chapter 2, I shared how fortunate Xactly was to have included language in our contracts allowing us to collect anonymized data. When we put this language into our contract, I figured about two-thirds of all clients would opt out, but, to my surprise, roughly 97 percent of our customers opted *in*. We didn't understand what a gift this was until years later when we began specifically designing products around that rich dataset to help our clients make meaning, gain insights, and drive action.

Here's the crucial part: although we didn't understand precisely *how* collecting all that data would help us in 2005, we were certain it would have value down the road. Today, it's the cornerstone of our business, and we see AI as the logical next step in that progression.

Why? Two words: actionable information. It's easy to ask a generative AI tool like ChatGPT a set of questions and receive a series of meaningful outputs in return. Moreover, through a collaborative relationship we refer to as the *human loop* (more on that a little bit later), these tools improve over time. The more questions you ask—and the better you get at asking them—the better answers you'll get. And while the current generation of AI tools can do this reasonably well, future tools will do this exceedingly well.

What will those future tools look like? It's still too early to say for sure. However, one thing is already clear: those who embrace AI tools and implement them effectively will have a tremendous advantage over their competitors.

Here in the final chapter of the book, we'll be exploring some of the different ways generative AI can help your revenue operation. Before we jump in, however, first let's do some level-setting: the value of AI is not in taking your company from zero to one hundred.

Just like in F1 racing, its value is in incremental gains. What would it look like if you could generate 2 to 5 percent more performance from every single rep in your business? How would your reps benefit from a tool that pattern matches their behaviors and works to keep them on track? What would it look like if your team no longer had to waste endless hours of rote work and spent more time making human connections with your customers?

These are the kinds of questions that will help your organization harness generative AI to do more with less. And make no mistake, those little gains add up. According to a recent MIT/ Stanford study, workers at a software firm that had access to generative AI tools were 14 percent more productive than those that didn't.[26] While that study was for organizations as a whole, imagine the impact those tools could have on your revenue operation. Here are a few of the changes we can already see coming.

THE HUMAN LOOP

Every day, sales reps in companies around the world start their days by looking at their territories and trying to determine who they're going to call. It's a painful process with no guaranteed payoff. Even if they do have some data to pull, it's usually both difficult to access and unreliable, leaving them to go off their guts.

Imagine if they had a generative AI to collaborate with. With just a simple voice command, they could prompt their tool to:

- Pull up their territory
- Filter out all recently closed deals
- Identify all publicly traded companies from the remaining dataset
- Scan all publicly available information on those remaining companies
- From that public information, identify companies who said certain keywords—especially in public comments on their most recent earnings report
- Identify the relevant stakeholders at those companies by specific criteria (e.g., VP level, with the company for two years, etc.)
- Write a series of intro letters to those stakeholders

---

26 Erik Brynjolfsson, Danielle Li, and Lindsey R. Raymond, "Generative AI at Work" (working paper 31161, National Bureau of Economic Research, April 2023), https://doi.org/10.3386/w31161.

Boom. Just like that, with just a few minutes spent thinking carefully about relevant criteria, your rep now knows exactly who they should be reaching out to—and they even have their intro letters ready to go too.

Are the letters perfect? Of course not. They're a first draft. But these first drafts just saved the rep a tremendous amount of time that would have otherwise been spent researching and drafting. Now, instead of doing the grunt work, they're free to focus on the fine-tuning work.

This is how generative AI works best: as part of a human loop. A human prompts the tool with a specific request, the AI tool creates a useful outline, and the human refines it. With each iteration, thanks to the combined wonders of human adaptation and machine learning, both the inputs and outputs become more refined, and the human loop grows stronger.

What does this mean in practice for the sales reps of today? Unfortunately for those hoping to get out of all the legwork, they're still going to spend some time refining their queries and editing the outputs. But given enough time, data, and effort, those prompts are only going to get better.

That's why I see the potential for a lot more than just a 14 percent gain in company productivity. The more you feed the program on the front end, the more time you gain on the back end. Instead of spending endless time on prospecting—a rote process that every rep I've ever known can't stand—they get to spend more time making contact with potential buyers. And not just potential buyers. The *right* potential buyers.

This is just one example, of course. But even from this one example, it's easy to see how the principles might apply to other areas of sales, such as lead generation or marketing.

EASY TO USE, HARD TO RESIST

A few weeks before writing this chapter, Xactly had an executive off-site. During the event, we conducted a "color analysis." Each member of the executive team was assigned a color—red, yellow, green, and blue—that corresponded to their inclination to use data to drive their decision-making. On one end of the spectrum, the reds are aggressive decision-makers who are less interested in data and more focused on driving action. On the other end of the spectrum, the blues are more data-driven. They want to go ten layers deep before making any decision.

It was a fun—and very revealing—exercise. Despite all my data evangelism, I was still a red! I guess you can take the person out of sales, but you can't take the sales out of the person.

However, in the world of generative AI, I would fully expect nearly every single color assignment to change for every member of the executive team. Why? Because generative AI tools are incredibly easy to use. Even an aggressive, deep-red sales rep has time to pull up a program and ask it a few questions before making a decision.

And to be clear, I mean you can literally just ask it a question—no typing or anything. There's no reason that tomorrow's AI tools won't resemble tools like Siri or Alexa.

Granted, we're not there yet. Xactly's AI-driven tool suite may be valuable, for instance, but historically that value has been limited; comp admins will define narrow data streams, arrange them on a dashboard, get specific insights from that data, and then take action. It's valuable, but it's limited.

Eventually, those tools will be more broadly available and more specifically applicable to a wider range of tasks. And when that day comes, people who today are more data-averse are going to start seeing and reaping the benefits of data, and they're going to love it.

BUT I DON'T WANT MY JOB REPLACED!

Inevitably, whenever anyone talks about AI in any form, someone raises the concern that, if we continue down this path, AI will come to take all of our jobs.

Will certain jobs go away as a result of AI? Probably. Historically, every new innovation has made certain types of work less relevant.

But I don't see that happening in sales. It's too uniquely human, it requires too much nuanced interpersonal interaction, and I don't see AI being able to even remotely approximate that anytime soon—if ever.

In fact, if anything, by eliminating or reducing the time spent on the mundane, administrative side of their work, AI frees up reps to do what they do best: be human.

As for the blues? Well, they're never going to be satisfied. Awash in this sea of valuable insights, they'll just keep asking for more. And we'll love them for it.

STANDARDIZING THE REST TO FOCUS ON THE BEST

Our services aren't exactly cookie-cutter. Every implementation requires at least some degree of customization. However, that customization represents, at most, 50 percent of the implementation. The rest is standard across all projects.

We aren't unique in this regard, of course. The same could be said for many companies, especially those in tech. But while the bulk of a company's implementations may be the same, when it comes time to building those implementations out for a client, most start from ground zero every time.

The generative AI of the future will be able to examine the previous hundred implementations, identify the best practices common to all of them, and get that implementation 50, 60, or even 70 percent of the way there.

Then, with the automated part out of the way, the human side of the team is free to focus on the hard part: configuring the implementation to precisely meet their clients' needs. Such a process would be quicker, more efficient, and less expensive for the client—all while enabling the implementation team to do better work.

This is just one application. A generative AI tool trained to identify best practices can find those best practices anywhere. Want to know what all the "tiger" sellers in your organization have in common? What is that special recipe of traits that makes them best in breed? Generative AI will not only be able to help you identify the core traits that all your top sellers exhibit, but it will also be able to help your team identify where their own strengths and weaknesses lie and what improvements they can make to their own processes.

AI OR DIE?

In times of economic uncertainty, CEOs are always the first to get squeezed at a company. Suddenly, their boards have them chasing their own tails trying to respond to unfavorable market conditions, to grow without burning cash, and, of course, to make money.

That's a tough line to walk. Sure, it can be done—you've literally just read an entire book on how to do it—but it's not something most CEOs are accustomed to doing.

When put in this situation, CEOs often turn to the same place: the expense sheet. Then, they begin asking an all-too-familiar question: Which SaaS vendors can they drop, which ones can they keep, and which ones they can combine?

THE EVER-EXPANDING IMPACT
OF INTELLIGENT REVENUE

Incentivization isn't limited to traditional sales alone. And if your incentivization tool is driven by machine learning and AI, then the sky's the limit; anything you can measure, you can reward. Here are a few examples from some past and present Xactly clients:

- Software
- Financial and business services
- Telecom and media
- Luxury retailers
- Hotels and other hospitality and service industries
- Logistics
- Manufacturing

The companies representing these different industries all use incentivization in different ways. Retailers incentivize service. Hospitality companies incentivize upsells. Manufacturing companies incentivize safe, timely deliveries.

The possibilities go on, but here's the point: any behavior you want to incentivize, whether it's dollar driven or culture driven, you can absolutely do with an Intelligent Revenue approach and the right tools to drive the process.

That makes sense. After all, if you can retain—or even improve—functionality all while reducing both costs and the number of vendors, why wouldn't you?

Now here's another question: If you're the CEO in this situation, which vendors are you going to cut—the siloed vendors that just do one thing, or the integrated vendors whose products are driven by AI and machine learning? Naturally, I'm biased, but I can't imagine there being much of a choice.

If you're a SaaS vendor who hasn't yet embraced data and AI, this question should give you pause. After all, it's not just about what tools you can adopt to get the most value for your business, but what tools you can *produce* that will do the same for others. If you don't want your own product or service to wind up on the chopping block, it's high time you consider what an AI-driven implementation might look like for your business.

GET OFF THE FENCE AND START HAVING FUN

I have been married to my wife, Marla, for over thirty years. Part of that success can be attributed to the fact that I sweat the details; at minimum, I mark every birthday, holiday, and special occasion with flowers and a card.

Don't tell my wife this (I want to surprise her when she reads this book), but recently, I've been getting a little assistance with these efforts: I've been using ChatGPT to write her a short poem along with the flowers and card. I provide the details—what anniversary this is, the fact that she likes puppies, etc.—and it spits out a damn impressive little piece in a matter of seconds. More importantly, my wife loves them and always comments on how thoughtful they are.

If you gave me three hours with the exact same details and parameters, I could maybe—*maybe*—churn out a poem as good. More likely, ChapGPT would still beat me. For me, then, using generative AI in this context is a win-win. I get to create a moving tribute to my wife that she loves, and I don't have to burn half my day to do it.

These sorts of opportunities exist for each of us every day. Think about how many activities exist during your typical week that are rote, that you're not good at, or that you just don't have time for that generative AI might be able to handle for you.

Now imagine a world where generative AI can take care of these activities for you.

What are you going to do with all that extra time?

INTELLIGENT REVENUE TUNE-UPS

→ What ways do you see generative AI impacting your business?

→ What processes and responsibilities would your sales team kill to have off their plates?

→ How else could you see AI impacting your life? For instance, do you also wish you had a shortcut to creating charming poems and enhancing your relationship?

CONCLUSION

TODAY, WE STAND AT A TIPPING POINT.

Right now, Intelligent Revenue sounds new and unproven. But the organizations who have adopted this approach have already given themselves a massive advantage over their competition—although it will be merely table stakes tomorrow.

Knowing that, here's my question to you: What are you waiting for?

The days of the unicorn are over. Why follow the herd and risk extinction when there's a better way?

I've seen too many good companies buckle under the pressure, chasing round after round of fundraising while ignoring that they had not built a sustainable foundation for growth.

Even if you're convinced your company is destined to become the next unicorn, an Intelligent Revenue approach is more likely to get you there. If you're going to drive growth, you need a fine-tuned revenue engine to get you there. That means:

- Ditching error-prone, manual spreadsheets and automating your systems

- Using cloud-based, empirical data to create an accurate forecast and go-to-market strategy
- Replacing the hero culture and creating a culture where everyone in your operation has a chance to be a star

Of course, you're the captain of your own ship. I can't make the call for you. We may all be in the same storm, but each of us must choose how we will navigate that storm for ourselves.

IF YOU COULD ONLY DO ONE THING...

Throughout this book, we examined several approaches within an Intelligent Revenue framework that will help you modernize your revenue, ditch the unicorn mindset, and focus on building a quality business based on EBITDA rather than valuation. You will get the most value out of an Intelligent Revenue approach when you have all these approaches working in tandem. However, that doesn't mean you need to adopt a full suite of new capabilities all at once.

In fact, I wouldn't recommend it. Think back to the Maturity Model in Chapter 3. It's going to take some time evangelizing a new approach at your company and adopting new tools for execution, and no one should pay for tools they don't need (although many businesses often do).

This begs the question: Which tool or strategy should you start with?

The answer: whichever one will move the needle for your business the fastest.

For most organizations, that's going to be getting your revenue operation off of spreadsheets and onto modern, automated, AI-driven tools (Chapter 4). From there, you will likely see the most value in updating your sales planning processes (Chapter

7) or your compensation (Chapter 5) or your incentivization structures (Chapter 6).

Whatever route you go, however, here's my advice: don't boil the ocean.

There is some urgency to get out of the Stone Age, but this isn't a race. If you try to do everything at once, you'll end up overwhelmed. It's better to slow down, start with the end in mind, and then make incremental progress through our Maturity Model. That way, rather than thinking in a siloed, fragmented way, you'll have a complete picture of the endgame and will be able to approach your tool adoption strategically. That's how you build lasting success.

Similarly, consider your vendors. Many SaaS companies offer solutions capable of performing the kinds of tasks described in this book. Very few, however, offer a full suite of products that integrate and talk to each other. If you're only looking for a comp tool, it might not matter as much which provider you choose. However, if you're looking for a comprehensive, integrated solution, do your homework. Understand which company can help you reach your endpoint, not just your starting point. That way, you'll end up with a solution of far more strategic value to your business.

Finally, be patient. You will see change quickly, but you won't see change overnight. Certain products are faster, while others take longer. From there, once you're up and running with your first tool, consider the timeline for adding to your tool chain.

OPPORTUNITY IS CALLING

Remember Cliff Young, the sixty-one-year-old farmer who won the ultramarathon from Chapter 5? He won because he didn't carry the self-limiting beliefs that his fellow competitors did. In your own revenue operation, much of what seems impossible today is only a matter of self-limiting beliefs. Those blinders separate the people who make a million dollars a year selling software from those who wash out, even when they both start with the same opportunity.

No doubt, you've probably felt like Cliff Young's competitors from time to time. Maybe you've dreaded going to work in the morning because you weren't sure if you could deliver or make the money you needed. Maybe you fought against a flawed system—and all the anxiety and negativity that came with it—simply because you didn't understand there was a different way.

If there is one lesson I want you to take from this book, it's that there is a different way—and it works.

The thing is, I know I can't appeal to the logical side of your brain. You don't need to be told that an automated, AI-driven tool is better than a spreadsheet, just like you don't need to be told that GPS is better than a foldable road map.

But it's not about logic. It's about the cavemen with the square wheel, too busy with their problems to look up and notice that a better way already exists.

So look up.

See the opportunity that's right there waiting for you.

Then, when you're ready, embrace it.

WE CAN HELP

As with any digital transformation, adopting an Intelligent Revenue framework takes time and dedication. Fortunately, you don't have to go it alone.

Through either online or onsite certification programs, the Xactly team can guide you through a series of self-paced training modules to ensure you have all the knowledge you need to bring Intelligent Revenue to your organization. And if your sales lead still needs convincing about whether it's worth it, we can help with that too.

To learn more, please visit: https://www.xactlycorp.com/unicorn-fallacy-chris-cabrera

ACKNOWLEDGMENTS

IT'S HARD TO IMAGINE XACTLY HAS BEEN IN OPERATION working to change the revenue game for eighteen years. It's even harder to imagine that it's already been nearly ten years since my first book. But, as I said in the acknowledgments to the first book, time isn't always easy for me to wrangle, and without the support, assistance, and contributions from the following people, this book may have taken much longer to come out.

To my family: Marla, my wife; Alexa and Cole; my son-in-law, Will; and our new grandchild, Georgia Rose. Watching our family continue to grow is the greatest pleasure and honor of my life.

To my previous boards, investors, and mentors: I am largely a product of your generous investment in me. And, to Chas Hoppe, Mikey Kershisnik, and the team at Scribe Media: you did a brilliant job of capturing not only my thoughts but also the tone and intent of how I wanted to deliver this work. Additionally, I want to thank Arnab Mishra and Mary Jo Rose who helped guide me throughout the process.

To everyone at Xactly, and to others who've inspired me along the way: thank you. I am grateful for your support.

ABOUT THE AUTHOR

CHRIS CABRERA is the Founder and CEO of Xactly. With more than two decades of successful senior management experience, Cabrera has led Xactly's innovation as a founder and CEO since 2005. Headquartered in Los Gatos, California, Xactly offers an award-winning suite of solutions for sales performance management, sales effectiveness, sales compensation, and sales forecasting. Since its inception, Xactly has been an industry leader, going public on the New York Stock Exchange in 2015. Xactly was acquired by Vista Equity Partners in 2017.

Cabrera has won numerous awards, including being named a Top SaaS CEO for three years running. He has been featured in *The Wall Street Journal* and *The New York Times* and is the author of *Game the Plan*, a popular book that helps business leaders understand sales. Cabrera was also named the "Alumni Entrepreneur of the Year" by the Lloyd Greif Center for Entrepreneurial Studies at the USC Marshall School of Business.

Shortly after founding Xactly, Cabrera established the XactlyOne Foundation, a nonprofit coordinating volunteer opportunities and projects for employees in local communities.

To date, XactlyOne has raised and donated hundreds of thousands of dollars and provided tens of thousands of volunteer hours to organizations in need.

Cabrera spends his spare time being creative and working on artistic projects such as river tables, paintings, pottery, and a variety of objects from different kinds of rare wood. He also has a vineyard and is a winemaker, plays golf, is an avid F1 fan, and loves being around his family and friends.

Printed in the USA
CPSIA information can be obtained
at www.ICGtesting.com
LVHW091311060324
773422LV00004B/7